The Origin And Permanent Value Of The Old Testament

Charles Foster Kent

The Origin And Permanent Value Of The Old Testament

I

THE ECLIPSE AND REDISCOVERY OF THE OLD TESTAMENT

The opening chapters of the Gospels record only three or four meagre facts regarding the first thirty years of Jesus' life. The real history of those significant years ran so far beneath the surface of external events that it completely escaped the historian. The history of the mental and spiritual life of the Master is recorded in his mature character and teachings. The fugitive hints, however, vividly illustrate the supreme fact that he ever grew stronger, becoming filled with wisdom; — and the grace of God was upon him (Luke ii. 40). They reveal a soul not only in closest touch with God and with human life, but also in eager quest for the vital truth regarding God and man recorded in the Scriptures of his race. It requires no imagination to picture the young Jew of Nazareth eagerly studying in the synagogue, at the temple, and alone by himself the sacred writings found in our Old Testament, for this fact is clearly recorded on every page of the Gospels.

The events of Hebrew history, and its heroes — Abraham, David, Elijah — were all familiar to him. The Old Testament was the background of a large portion of the Sermon on the Mount. From Deuteronomy vi. 4, 5, and Leviticus xix. 18 he drew his marvellous epitome of all law and duty. In the wisdom literature, and especially in the book of Proverbs, he found many of those practical truths which he applied to life with new authority and power. From the same storehouse of crystallized experience he derived certain of those figures which he expanded into his inimitable parables; he adopted also, and put to new use, the effective gnomic form of teaching of the wisdom school. As in the mouth of his herald, John the Baptist, the great moral and spiritual truths, first proclaimed by the ancient prophets, live again on the lips of Jesus. At every point in his teachings one recognizes the thought and language of the older Scriptures. At the moments of his greatest temptation and distress, even in the last agony, the words of the ancient law and psalms were on his lips and their consoling and inspiring messages in his mind.

What is so strikingly true of Jesus is equally true of the apostles and disciples who have given us the New Testament books: the atmosphere in which they lived, the thoughts which they thought, and the language in which they spoke, were those of the Old Testament. Not bowing slavishly before it, as did their Jewish contemporaries, but with true reverence, singling out that which was vital and eternal, they made it the basis of their own more personal and perfect message to humanity. But for them, and for the early Church, until at least the middle of the second Christian century, the only scriptures regarded as authoritative were those of the Old Testament. Even then, only gradually, and under the pressure of real needs, were different groups of Christian writings added and ascribed an authority equal to that of the older Scriptures.

Throughout the Middle Ages and in the eyes of the Protestant reformers the two great divisions of the Bible continued to command equal respect and attention. From the Old Testament and its reflection in the teachings of Paul, Puritanism and the theology of the past three centuries derived most of that which revealed their strength as well as their weakness. From the law, the prophets, and the book of Proverbs they drew their stern spirit of justice, their zeal for righteousness, and their uncompromising condemnation of everything that seemed to them wrong. Their preachers nobly echoed the thunders of Sinai and the denunciations of an Elijah, an Amos, and an Hosea. They often failed, however, to recognize the divine love which prompted the stern words of the prophets, and to see that these denunciations and warnings were simply intended to arouse the conscience of the people and to make them worthy of the rich blessings that God was eager to bestow. Misinterpretation of the spirit of the later Old Testament reformers, who dramatically portrayed Jehovah's hatred for the abominable heathen cults in the form of commands to slaughter the peoples practising them, frequently led the Puritan fathers to treat their foes in a manner neither biblical nor Christian. To this narrow interpretation of the letter rather than the spirit of the Old Testament, and the emphasis placed upon its more primitive and imperfect teachings can be directly traced the worst faults of that courageous band who lived and died fighting for what they conceived to be truth and right.

It is undoubtedly true that during the past two decades the Old Testament has in fact, if not in theory, been assigned to a secondary place in the life and thought of Christendom. This is not due to the fact that the Christ has been exalted to his rightful position of commanding authority and prestige. All that truly exalts him likewise exalts the record of the work of his forerunners which he came to bring to complete fulfilment and upon which he placed his eternal seal of approval. Rather, the present eclipse of the Old Testament appears to be due to three distinct causes. The first is connected with the reaction from Puritanism, and especially from its false interpretation of the Bible. Against intolerance and persecution the heart of man naturally rebelled. These rang true neither with life nor the teaching of Jesus. Refuge from the merciless and seemingly flawless logic of the earlier theologians was found in the simple, reassuring words of the Gospels. The result was that, with the exception of a very few books like the Psalter, the Old Testament, which was the arsenal of the old militant theology, has been unconsciously, if not deliberately, shunned by the present generation.

Within the past decade this tendency has been greatly accelerated by the work of the so-called "Higher Critics." Because it presents more literary and historical problems, and because it was thought, at first, to be farther away from the New Testament, the citadel of the Christian faith, the Old Testament has been the scene of their greatest activity. With what seemed to the onlooker to be a supreme disregard for the traditions long accepted as established by the Church, they have persistently applied to the ancient Scriptures the generally accepted canons and methods of modern historical and literary study. In their scientific zeal they have repeatedly overturned what were once regarded as fundamental dogmas. Unfortunately the first reports of their work suggested that it was only destructive. The very foundations of faith seemed to be shaking. Sinai appeared to be enveloped in a murky fog, instead of the effulgence of the divine glory; Moses seemed to become a vague, unreal figure on the distant horizon of history; David's voice only faintly echoed through the Psalter; and the noblest messages of prophet, sage, and psalmist were anonymous.

Little wonder that many who heard only from afar the ominous reports of the digging and delving, and vague rumors,—all the more terrifying because vague,—either leaped to the conclusion that the authority of the Old Testament had been undermined or else rallied in a frantic effort to put a stop, by shouting or compulsion, to the seemingly sacrilegious work of destruction. When the history of the Higher Criticism of the Old Testament is finally written, it will be declared most unfortunate that the results first presented to the rank and file of the Christian Church were, as a rule, largely negative and in many cases relatively unimportant. In their initial enthusiasm for scientific research scholars, alas! sometimes lost the true perspective and failed to recognize relative values. The date, for example, of Isaiah xl.-lv. is important for the right understanding and interpretation of these wonderful chapters, but its value is insignificant compared with the divine messages contained in these chapters and their direct application to life. Moreover, instead of presenting first the testimony and then patiently pointing out the reasonableness and vital significance of the newer conclusions, scholars sometimes, under the influence of their convictions, made the fatal mistake of enunciating those conclusions simply as dogmas.

History demonstrates that established religions and churches always hold tenaciously to old doctrines, and therefore regard new conclusions with suspicion. This tendency is clearly illustrated in the experience of Jesus; for with all his divine tact and convincing authority, he was not able to win the leaders of Judaism to the acceptance of his revolutionizing teachings. Yet one cannot escape the conviction that if in this age of enlightenment and open-mindedness, the positive results of modern scholarship had been presented first, this latest chapter in God's revelation of himself to man would have been better understood and appreciated by the leaders of the Church, and its fruits appropriated by those whose interests are fixed on that which is of practical rather than theoretical import. At least many open-minded people might have been saved from the supreme error of writing, either consciously or unconsciously, Ichabod across the pages of their Old Testament.

The third reason why the Old Testament has suffered temporary eclipse in so many minds is more fundamental; it is because of the difficulties in understanding it. The background of the New Testament is the Roman world and a brief century with which we Western readers are well acquainted; but the background of the Old is the ancient East—the age and land of wonder, mystery, and intuition, far removed from the logical, rushing world in which we live. The Old Testament contains a vast and complex literature, filled with the thoughts and figures and cast in the quaint language of the Semitic past. Between us and that past there lie not merely long centuries, but the wide gulf that is fixed between the East and the West.

With three such distinct and powerful currents—reaction, suspicion, and misunderstand—bearing us from the Old Testament, it might be predicted that in a decade or two it would lie far behind our range of vision. Other forces however are, in divine providence, rapidly bringing it back to us again, so that we are able to understand and appreciate it as never before since the beginning of the Christian era. The chasm between us and it is really being bridged rather than broadened. The long centuries that lie back of the Old Testament have suddenly been illuminated by great search-lights, so that today we are almost as well acquainted with them as with the beginning of the Christian era. From ancient monuments have arisen, as from the dead, an army of contemporary witnesses, sometimes confirming, sometimes correcting, but at all times marvellously supplementing the biblical data. Now the events and characters of Old Testament history no longer stand alone in mysterious isolation, but we can study in detail their setting and real significance. At every point the biblical narrative and thought are brought into touch with real life and history. The biographies and policies, for example, of Sennacherib and Cyrus, are almost as well known as those of Napoleon and Washington. The prophets are not merely voices, but men with a living message for all times, because they primarily dealt with the conditions and needs of their own day. The vital relation and at the same time the infinite superiority of the religious teachings of the Old Testament to those of earlier ages and peoples are clearly revealed.

Interpreted in the light of contemporary literature and language, most of the obscurities of the Old Testament melt away. Modern research in the fields of Semitic philology and syntax and the discovery of older texts and versions have put into the hands of translators new and valuable tools for making clear to all the thoughts in the minds of the original writers of the Old Testament. Studies in comparative religion, geography, and modern Oriental life and customs have illuminated and illustrated at every point the pages of the ancient writings. To utilize all these requires time and devotion, but he who is willing to study may know his Old Testament to-day as well as he does the New.

Fully commensurate with the great light that has been shed upon it from without, is that which has come from a careful study of the testimony of the Old Testament itself. Until recent times the Church has been content to accept blindly the traditions of the late Jewish rabbis regarding the origin, history, and interpretation of their scriptures. Handed down through the Church Fathers and interwoven with creeds and popular beliefs, they have been identified in many minds with the teaching of the Bible itself. Yet, when we analyze their origin and true character, we find that many of them have absolutely no support in the Scriptures, and in many cases are directly contradictory to the plain biblical teachings. Too often they are but the fanciful conjectures of the rabbis. Developed in an uncritical age, and based upon the unreliable methods of interpretation current among the Jews in the early Christian centuries, they are often sadly misleading. A close analogy is found in the traditional identifications of most of the Palestinian sacred sites. To-day the Oriental guide shows the skull of Adam beneath the spot where tradition places the cross of Christ. If the traveller desires, he will point out the very stones which Jesus declared God could raise up to be children of Abraham. Every question which curiosity or genuine interest has raised is answered by the seemingly authoritative voice of tradition. Investigation, however, proves that almost all of these thousand identifications are probably incorrect. The discovery is a shock to the pious imagination; but to the healthy mind uncertainty is always better than error. Furthermore, uncertainty often proves the door which leads to established truth.

Even so the modern historical and critical spirit has led men to turn from the generally accepted but exceedingly doubtful rabbinical traditions regarding, for example, the date and authorship of many of the Old Testament books, to the authoritative evidence found in those writings themselves. In this they are but following the example of the Great Teacher, who repeatedly appealed from the same rabbis and their misleading traditions to the same ancient Scriptures. The saddest fact is that many of his followers, even to-day, hesitate to follow his inspired leadership. Fortunately, as the varied, strata and formations of the rocks tell the story of the earth's early history, so these early writings furnish the data for reconstructing the illuminating history of their origin, growth, and transmission. Often the testimony of the facts differs as widely from the familiar inherited traditions as the conclusions of modern science from the vague guesses of primitive man regarding the riddles of existence. Neither may represent absolute and final truth, and yet no serious-minded man can question which is really the more authoritative. To-day one of the most vital issues before the Christian. Church is whether it will follow the guidance of its Founder and accept the testimony of the Bible itself or cling blindly to the traditions of the rabbis and Church Fathers.

The student of history at once recognizes in the modern movement, of which the watchword is, "Back to the testimony of the Bible," the direct sequel to the Protestant Reformation. The early reformers took the chains off the Bible and put it into the hands of men, with full permission to study and search. Vested interests and dogmatism soon began to dictate how it should be studied and interpreted, and thus it was again placed practically under lock and key. It is an interesting fact that a young Zulu chief, a pupil of Bishop Colenso of South Africa, first aroused the Anglo-Saxon world to the careful, fearless, and therefore truly reverential study of its Old Testament. With this new impetus, the task of the Reformers was again taken up, and in the same open, earnest spirit. For two generations it has commanded the consecrated energies of the most thorough scholars of Christendom. Those of England, Scotland, Ireland, France, Germany, Austria, Switzerland, Norway, Sweden, America, and Canada have worked shoulder to shoulder, dividing the work, carefully collecting and classifying the minutest data, comparing results, and, on the basis of all this work, formulating conclusions, some assured and some hypothetical, which best explain the facts.

Often, to those who have not followed the detailed steps, these conclusions have seemed only destructive. Many of them are assuredly so; but the vital question which every honest man should ask is, Do they destroy the Bible, or simply the false traditions that have gathered about it? Fortunately, most of the leaders of the Church and most intelligent laymen have already discerned the only emphatic answer to this question. The Church is undoubtedly passing quietly through a revolution in its conception and attitude toward the Bible, more fundamental and far-reaching than that represented by its precursor the Protestant Reformation; but its real significance is daily becoming more apparent. Not a grain of truth which the Bible contains has been destroyed or permanently obscured. Instead, the débris of time-honored traditions and dogmas have been cleared away, and the true Scriptures at last stand forth again in their pristine splendor.

Freed from the misconceptions and false traditions which have gathered about it, the true Old Testament rises from amidst the dust and din of the much digging and delving. To those who have known only the old it is a fresh revelation. Its literary beauty, its naturalness, its dignity, its majestic authority are a surprise to those who have not followed its unveiling. The old vagueness and mystery have in part disappeared, and instead it is found to contain a thousand vital, living messages for to- day. Its human as well as its divine qualities command our interest and attention. Through it all God speaks with a new clearness and authority. Thus, that which we thought was dead has risen, and lives again to inspire us to noble thought and deed and service.

II

THE REAL NATURE AND PURPOSE OF THE OLD TESTAMENT

Turning from the Jewish and mediæval traditions and theories which so easily beset us, we ask, What is the real nature of the Old Testament as it is revealed in this new and clearer light? The first conclusion is that it is a library containing a large and complex literature, recording the varied experiences, political, social, ethical, and religious, of the Israelitish race. The fact that it is a library consisting of many different books is recognized by the common designation of the two testaments. As is well known, our English word Bible came originally from the Papyrus or Byblus reed, the pith of which was widely used in antiquity as the material from which books were made. It was natural, therefore, that in the Greek a little book should be designated as a biblion. About the middle of the second Christian century the Greek Christians (first in the so-called Second Epistle of Clement xlv. 2) began to call their sacred scriptures, Ta Biblia, the books. When this title was transferred to the Latin it was, by reason of a natural and yet significant error, treated as a feminine singular, Biblia, which, reappears In English as Bible. This most appropriate name emphasizes the fact that the books thus described are a unit and yet a collection of little books, selected from a larger literature and given their present position of preeminent authority.

The term Testament suggests not the form and authority of the books, but their theme. It is the English translation, through the Latin and Greek, of the Hebrew word,berîth, usually rendered, covenant. It means a bond or basis of agreement. It implies a close and binding contract between two parties, and defines the terms to which each subscribes and the obligations which they thus assume. The Old Covenant or Testament, therefore, is primarily the written record of the origin, terms, and history of the solemn agreement which existed between the Israelitish nation and Jehovah. The early narratives preserve the traditions of its origin; the lawgivers endeavored to define its terms and the obligations that rested upon the people; the prophets interpreted them in the life of the nation, and the sages into the life of the individual; and the historical books recorded its practical working. The significant fact is that back of the Old Testament records exists something greater and deeper than pen can fully describe: it is a vital, living connection between Jehovah and his people that makes possible the unique relation which finds expression in the remarkable history of the race and in the experiences and souls of its spiritual leaders. Thus through life, and in the concrete terms of life, God reveals himself to the life of humanity.

In the light of this truth the Jewish and medieval dogma that every word, and even every letter of Scripture, was directly dictated by God himself, seems sadly mechanical and bears the marks of the narrow schools of thought in which it took form. Hebrew was not, and probably will never be, the language of heaven! Not on skins and papyrus rolls, but in the life of the Israelitish race and on the minds and consciences of enlightened men, God wrote his revelation. History and the character and consciousness of the human race are its imperishable records. Fortunately he also aroused certain men of old, not by word and act only, but by the pen as well, to record the revelation that was being perfected in the life of their nation and in their own minds and hearts. He did not, however, dictate to them the form of their writings nor vouch for their verbal inerrancy. In time, out of their writings were gradually collected and combined the most significant passages and books, and to these was finally attributed the authority that they now rightfully enjoy.

The ultimate basis of that authority, however, is not their presence in the canon of the Old Testament. At the same time their presence there is deeply significant, for it represents the indorsement of many ages and of countless thousands who, from the most varied points of view and amid the most diverse experiences, have tested and found these ancient scriptures worthy of the exalted position that has gradually been assigned to them. It is not the support of the Church, although this also for the same reason is exceedingly significant. It is not the calm assumption, of authority that appears at every point throughout the Old Testament, although this is richly suggestive; the sacred writings of other religions make even more pretentious claims. It is not that its commands and doctrines come from the mouths of great prophets and priests, like Moses, Samuel, Isaiah, and Jeremiah. This fact undoubtedly had great weight with those who formed the final canon of the Old Testament, and the authority of a strong, noble personality is supremely impressive; but divine authority never emanates primarily from a man, however great be his sanctity. Furthermore, to establish the authority derived from a Moses or a Samuel it is necessary in every case to prove that the books attributed to them by late tradition actually came from their pens. Even if this could in every case be done, some of the noblest passages in the Old Testament remain avowedly anonymous; for the tendency of the great majority of its authors was clearly to send forth their messages without any attempt to associate their own names with them.

The ultimate authority of the Old Testament, therefore, is not dependent upon devoted canon-makers, nor the weighty testimony of the Church, nor upon its own claims, nor the reputation of the inspired men who have written it, nor the estimate of any age. Its seat of authority is more fundamental. It contains the word of God because it faithfully records and interprets the most important events in the early religious history of man, and simply and effectively presents God's revelation of himself and of his will in the minds and hearts of the great pre-Christian heralds of ethical and spiritual truth. Back of the Old Testament is a vast variety of vital experiences, national and individual, political and spiritual, social and ethical, pleasurable and painful. Back of all these deeply significant experiences is God himself, through them making known his character and laws and purpose to man.

Students of the rediscovered Old Testament also recognize, in the light of a broader and more careful study, the fact, so often and so fatally overlooked in the past, that its authority lies not in the field of natural science, nor even of history in the limited sense. Time and patience were destined to increase man's knowledge in these great departments and also to develop his mind in attaining it. The teaching of the Old Testament is authoritative only in the far more important realm of ethics and religion. Paul truly voiced its supreme claim when he said that it was profitable for teaching, for reproof, for correction, for instruction in righteousness, that the man of God may be perfect, completely fitted for every good work (II Tim. iii. 16, 17). The assertion by the Church in the past of claims nowhere made or implied by the Old Testament itself is unfortunately still a fertile source of perplexity and dissension to many faithful souls. Their salvation is to be found in a clear and intelligent appreciation of the real nature and claim of these ancient writings.

One dominant aim determines the form of each book and the selection of individual passages and binds together the whole: it is effectively to set forth spiritual truth and to mould in accordance with God's will the characters and beliefs of men. It was the supreme bond that bound together prophets, priests, sages, and psalmists, although the means by which they accomplished their common purpose differed widely. Many a current tradition, and the crude conceptions of the ancients regarding the natural world, are recorded in the Old Testament; but they are not there merely to perpetuate history nor to increase the total of scientific knowledge, but rather because they concretely illustrate and impress some vital ethical and spiritual truth. Such singleness of religious purpose is paralleled nowhere else except in the work and teachings of Jesus and his apostles.

The ever-present evidence of the divine authority back of the spiritual teachings of the Old Testament as a whole is that they ring true to life and meet its needs. By their fruits we know them. It is the demonstration of the laboratory. We know that they are inspired because they inspire. The principles underlying the social sermons of Amos are as applicable to present conditions as when first uttered. The sooner they are practically applied the sooner our capitalistic civilization can raise its head now bowed In shame. The faith that breathes through the Psalms is the faith that upholds men to-day in the midst of temptation and trial. The standards of justice, tempered by love, which are maintained in the Old Testament laws make good citizens both of earth and heaven. As long as men continue to test the teachings of the Old Testament scriptures in the laboratory of experience and to know them by their fruits, nothing can permanently endanger their position in the Christian Church or in the life of humanity. Neglect and indifference, not Higher Criticism, alone permanently threaten the authority of the Old Testament as well as that of the New.

Recognizing the real nature and purpose of these ancient records, the true student neither denies nor is disturbed by the marks of their human authorship. As in the case of the Gospels, the variations between the parallel narratives are all evidence of their genuineness and of the sincerity of their purpose. They demonstrate that God's revelation is adapted to the needs of life and the comprehension of man, because it was through life and expressed in the terms of life. Their individual peculiarities and minor errors often introduce us more intimately to the biblical writers and help us to understand more clearly and sympathetically their visions of truth and of God. Above all, they teach us to look ever through and beyond all these written records to the greater revelation, which they reflect, and to the infinite Source of all knowledge and truth.

The inconsistencies and imperfect teachings which are revealed by a critical study of the Old Testament are also but a few of the many indices that it is the record of a gradually unfolding revelation. Late Jewish tradition, which is traceable even in the Old Testament itself, was inclined to assign the origin of everything which it held dear to the very beginnings of Hebrew history, and in so doing it has done much to obscure its true genesis. Fortunately, however, the history of God's gradual training of the race was writ too plainly in the earlier Old Testament scriptures to be completely obscured by later traditions. The recognition that God's all-wise method of revealing spiritual as well as scientific truth was progressive, adapted to the unfolding consciousness of each succeeding age, at once sweeps away many of the greatest difficulties that have hitherto obscured the true Old Testament. Jesus with his divine intuition appreciated this principle of growth. Unhesitatingly he abrogated certain time-honored Old Testament laws with the words, Ye have heard that it was said ... but I say to you. His own interpretation of his relation to the sacred writings of his race was that he came to bring them to complete fulfilment. Rearranged in their approximately chronological order, the Old Testament books become the harmonious and many-sided record of ten centuries of strenuous human endeavor to know and to do the will of God and of his full and gracious response to that effort. The beatitude of those who hunger and thirst after righteousness was as true in the days of Moses as it was when Jesus proclaimed it.

Finally, the right and normal attitude toward the Old Testament leads to the wholesome conclusion that its different books are of very different values. The great critic of Nazareth again set the example. As we have just seen, certain of the Old Testament laws he distinctly abrogated; others he quietly ignored; others, as, for example, the law of love (Deut. vi. 5, and Lev. xix. 19) he singled out and gave its rightful place of central authority. A careful study of the Gospels, in the light of the Old Testament, demonstrates that a very important element in his work, as the Saviour of men, was in thus separating the dross in the older teachings from the gold, and then in giving to the vital truth a clearer, more personal, and yet more universal application. For the intelligent student and teacher of to-day the Old Testament still remains a great mine of historical, ethical, and religious truth. Some parts, like Genesis, Deuteronomy, Hosea, Jeremiah, Isaiah xl.-lv., and the Psalter, are richly productive. Others, like Numbers, Chronicles, and Esther, are comparatively barren.

Since the Old Testament is the record of a progressively unfolding revelation, it is obvious that all parts do not possess an equal authority. To place the example of the patriarchs or of David, who lived when ethical standards and religious beliefs were only partially developed, on an equality with the exalted ideals of the later prophets, is to misinterpret those ancient Scriptures and to reject the leadership of the Great Teacher. At the same time, studied from the newer point of view, the examples of those early heroes are found to illustrate vital principles in human life and to inspire and warn the child of to-day as effectively as they did far back in the childhood of the race.

In these later days God has taken the Bible from the throne of infallibility on which Protestantism sought to place it. By a gradual yet benign process, which we were nevertheless at first inclined bitterly to resent, he has opened our eyes to its true character and purpose. Again, he has pronounced his Thou shall not to the natural and yet selfish human desire to transfer moral and intellectual responsibility from the individual conscience to some external authority. Again, he has told us that only in the sanctuary of the human soul is the Infallible One to be found. Yet in order that we each may find him there, the cumulative religious experience of the countless thousands who have already found him is of inestimable value. The Old Testament contains not merely the word of God, but, together with its complement the New, is the great guide-book in finding and knowing him, It blazes the way which, the pilgrim of to-day, as in the past, must follow from his cradle to the throne of God. At each point it is richly illustrated by the actual religious experiences of real men and women. Their mistakes and their victories, are equally instructive. From many vantage-points reached by prophets and priests and psalmists, we are able to catch new and glorious visions of God's character and purpose for mankind. Through its pages—sometimes dimly, sometimes brightly, But growing ever clearer—shines the giving light of God's truth and revelation, culminating in the Christ, the perfected revelation and the supreme demonstration that man, though beset by temptation, baffled by obstacles, deserted by friends, and maligned by foes, can nevertheless, by the invincible sword of love and self-sacrifice, conquer the world and become one with God, as did the peerless Knight of Nazareth.

III

THE EARLIEST CHAPTERS IN DIVINE REVELATION

Since the days of the Greek philosophers the subject of inspiration and revelation has been fertile theme for discussion and dispute among scholars and theologians. Many different theories have been advanced, and ultimately abandoned as untenable. In its simplest meaning and use, inspiration describes the personal influence of one individual upon the mind and spirit of another. Thus we often say, "That man inspired me." What we are or do under the influence of that intellectual or spiritual impulse is the effect and evidence of the inspiration. Similarly, divine inspiration is the influence of God's spirit or personality upon the mind and spirit of man. It may find expression in an exalted emotional state, in an heightened clarity of mental perception, in noble deeds, in the development of character, indeed in a great variety of ways; but its seat is always the mind of man and its ultimate cause the Deity himself.

The early Old Testament expression most commonly used to describe inspiration was that the Spirit of God rushed upon the man, as it did upon Saul, causing him to burst forth into religious ecstasy or frenzy (I Sam. x. 6, 10), and upon Samson, giving him great bodily strength or prowess in war (Judg. xiv. 6, 19, xv. 14). Skill in interpreting dreams and in ruling was also regarded as evidence that the Spirit of God was in a man like Joseph (Gen. xli. 38); but above all the prophetic gift was looked upon as the supreme evidence of the presence of the Spirit of Jehovah (Hos. ix. 1; Micah ii. 7, iii. 8). The word spirit as thus used in the Old Testament is exceedingly suggestive. It means primarily the breath, that comes from the nostrils. Though invisible to the eye, the breath was in the thought of primitive man the symbol of the active life of the individual. In the full vigor of bodily strength or in violent exercise it came quick and strong; in times of weakness it was faint; when it disappeared, death ensued; the living personality was gone, and only the play remained. The same Hebrew word, rúach, described the wind — unseen, intangible, and yet one of the most real and irresistible forces in all the universe. Thus it was a supremely appropriate term to describe the activity of God, as it produced visible effects in the minds and lives of men. In the later Old Testament literature its use was extended, so that to the Spirit of God was ascribed activity in the natural world and in human history.

Of the two terms, revelation is broader than inspiration. Sometimes it is used collectively, to designate the truth revealed, but it more properly describes the means or process whereby it is made apparent to the human mind. It implies that truth is always existent, but only gradually recognized. Inspiration is one of the chief means whereby the human vision is clarified so as to perceive it. Natural phenomena, environment, and above all experience, are also mighty agents in making the divine character and truth clear to the mind of man. The author of the Epistle to the Hebrews declares, with true insight, that God spoke in divers manners. All the universe, all history, and all life reveal him and his ultimate truths, for each is effective in opening the mental and spiritual eye of man to see the realm long awaiting him as conqueror.

For countless ages electricity has inscribed its magic tracery on the storm-cloud and performed its all-important functions in organic life, but not until men's eyes were opened by experience and trained observation to recognize its laws, was it practically applied to the needs of civilization. Similarly, unchanging moral and spiritual laws have existed through all time, but they have not become operative in human life until the eye of some seer is opened by a great experience, or under the direct influence of the Spirit of God he is led to see and proclaim them. Thus God is in all and reveals himself through all nature and life, but it is only through the mind and on the lips of his highest creature, man, that truth is fully appreciated, formulated, and applied.

In the broader sense all revelation is divine, for it reveals God and his laws; and yet it is obvious that there is a real difference between the revelation recorded in a scientific book and that of the Bible. It is a difference both in subject-matter and in the ends to which the truth thus made manifest shall be applied. The one relates to the objective world, the world of things; the other relates to human beliefs, emotions, and acts.

Moreover, it is evident that the spiritual revelation which is in part recorded in the Bible was not limited to the Israelitish race or to the twelve centuries represented by the Old and New Testaments. The biblical writers themselves assume this fact. According to the early Judean prophetic narratives, Enoch, who lived ages before Abraham and Moses, was a worshipper of Jehovah (Gen. iv. 26). Cain and Abel are both represented in the familiar story of Genesis iv., as bringing their offerings to Jehovah. One of the chief teachings of the earliest stories in the Old Testament is that men from the first knew and worshipped God and were held responsible for their acts according to their moral enlightenment. History, science, and the Bible unite in testifying that the revelation of spiritual truth to mankind was something gradual, progressive, and cumulative; also that it is dependent upon the ability of men to receive it. This capacity of the individual to receive is, after all, the determining factor in the process of divine revelation; for God's truth and his desire to impart it are always the same. Hence, whenever conditions favor, or national or private experiences clarify the vision of a race or group of men, a revelation is assured.

In the light of ancient history and the result of recent excavations it is possible, now as never before, to study the varied influences and forces employed by God in the past to open the spiritual eyes of mankind to see him and his truth. The geological evidence suggests that man, as man, has lived on this earth, fifty, perhaps one hundred thousand years. Anthropology, going farther back than history or primitive tradition, traces the slow and painful stages by which early man learned his first lessons in civilization and religion. From the beginning, man's instincts as a religious being have asserted themselves, crude though their expression was. The oldest mounds of Babylonia and Egypt contain ruins of ancient temples, altars, and abundant evidence of the religious zeal of the peoples who once inhabited these lauds. The earliest examples of human literature thus far discovered are largely religious in theme and spirit.

All these testify that early man believed in a power or powers outside himself, and that his chief passion was to know and do the will of his god or gods. Jesus himself bore witness in the opening words of the prayer which he taught his disciples, that this is the essence of religion. It was natural and inevitable that primitive man, with his naive view of the universe, should believe not in one but in many forces or spirits, and that he should first enthrone the physical above the ethical and spiritual. It is the instinctive tendency of the child to-day. The later identification of the divine powers with the sun, that gave light and fertility to the soil, or with the moon, that guided the caravans by night over the arid deserts, or with the other heavenly bodies, that moved in majestic array across the midnight sky, was likewise a natural step in the evolution of primitive belief.

Civilization and religion in antiquity developed, as a rule, side by side. The two great rivers, the Tigris and the Euphrates, commanding the trade of the north and the south; proximity to the desert with its caravans of traders going back and forth from the Euphrates to the Nile; the rich alluvial soil, which supported a dense population when properly drained and cultivated; and the necessity of developing in a higher degree the arts of defence in order to maintain the much contested territory, — these were a few of the many conditions that made ancient Babylonia one of the two earliest if not the oldest centre of human civilization. The commercial habits and the abundance of the plastic clay, which could easily be moulded into tablets for the use of the scribe, also fostered the early development of the literary art. The durability of the clay tablets and the enveloping and protecting qualities of the ruined mounds of ancient Babylonia have preserved in a marvellous way its early literature. The result is that we can now study, on the basis of contemporary documents, this early and yet advanced chapter in that divine revelation, the later culmination of which is recorded in the Bible.

It begins as far back of Moses as he is removed from us in point of time. Its political background at first is the little city states of Babylonia, each with its independent organization and its local schools of artists, whose products in many respects surpass anything that comes from the hands of later Semitic craftsmen. Each city had its temple, at which the patron god of the local tribe and district was worshipped. In some places it was the moon god Sin, as at Haran and Ur beside the desert; elsewhere, as at Nippur, Bel, or at Eridu near the Persian Gulf, Ea, the god of the great deep, was revered. In the name of the local deity offerings were brought, hymns were sung, and traditions were treasured, which extolled his might. The life of these little city states centred about the temple and its cult. To make it more glorious the artisans vied with each other, and the kings made campaigns that they might dedicate the spoils to the deity.

In time, perhaps as early as 4000 B.C., certain more energetic and ambitious kings succeeded in conquering neighboring cities; they even broadened their boundaries until they ruled over great empires extending to the Mediterranean on the west and the mountains of Elam on the east. In the name of the local god, each went forth to fight, and to him was attributed the glory of the victory. Naturally, when the territory of a city state grew into an empire, the god of that city was proclaimed and acknowledged as supreme throughout all the conquered territory. At the same time the local deities of the conquered cities continued to be worshipped at their ancient sanctuaries, and many a conquering king won the loyalty of his subjects by making a rich offering to the god and at the temple of a vanquished foe.

The logical and inevitable result of political union was the development of a pantheon, modelled after the imperial court, with the god of the victorious city at its head and the leading deities of the other cities in subordinate positions. When, during the latter part of the third millennium before Christ, Babylon's supremacy was permanently established under the rule of Hammurabi. Marduk, the god of that city, was thus placed at the head of the Babylonian pantheon. The theologians of the day also recast and combined the ancient legends, as, for example, those of the creation, so as to explain why he, one of the later gods, was acknowledged by all as supreme. A relationship was also traced between the leading gods, and their respective functions were clearly defined. Corresponding to each male deity was a female deity: thus, the consort of Marduk was Ishtar, while that of Bel was Belit. Furthermore, the ancient myths appear to have been, coördinated, so that from this time on Babylonian, theology presents a certain unity and symmetry, although one is constantly reminded of the very different elements out of which it had been built up.

Parallel to the evolution of Babylonian religion was that unfolding of ethical ideals and laws which finds its noblest record and expression in the remarkable code of Hammurabi (about 2250 B.C.). In its high sense of justice; in its regard for the rights of property and of individuals; in its attitude toward women, even though it comes from the ancient East; and above all in its protection of widows and orphans, this code marks almost as high a stage in the revelation of what is right as the primitive Old Testament laws, with which it has points of striking resemblance.

The evolution of ancient Egyptian civilization and religion was parallel at almost every stage with that of Babylonia, only in the dreamy land of the Nile the pantheon and the vast body of variant myths were never so thoroughly coördinated. The result is that its religion forever remains a labyrinth. Since all interest centred about the future life, instead of commercial pursuits, there is no evidence that the Egyptians ever produced a legal code at all comparable with that of Hammurabi. They did, however, develop a doctrine of sin which anticipates that of the Hebrew prophets. While the Babylonians conceived of sin as simply the failure to bring offerings, or to observe the demands of the ritual, or, in general, to pay proper homage to the gods, the Egyptians held that each individual was answerable, not only to the state, but also to the gods, for his every act and thought.

If they admitted of a comparison, it would be safe to say that the Babylonian religion and law in the days of Hammurabi were as far removed from the crude belief in spirits and the barbarous cults and practices of primitive man as the teachings of Jesus were from those of the kingly Babylonian lawgiver and his priestly advisers. Humanity's debt is exceedingly great to the thousands of devoted souls who, in ancient Babylonia and Egypt, according to their dim light, groped for God and the right. In part they found what they sought, although they never ceased to look through, a glass darkly.

The sad and significant fact is that from the days of Hammurabi to those of Nebuchadrezzar, Babylonian religion, law, and ethics almost entirely ceased to develop. No other great kings with prophetic insight appear to have arisen to hold up before the nation the principles of justice and mercy and true piety, The old superstitions and magic also continued in Babylonia as in Egypt to exercise more and more their baneful influence. Saddest of all the priesthood and ceremonialism, which had already reached a point of development commensurate and strikingly analogous to that of later Judaism, became the dominant power in the state, and defined religion not in terms of life and action, but of the ritual, and so constricted it that all true growth was impossible. Hence the religions of the Babylonians and Egyptians perished, like many others, because they ceased to grow, and therefore degenerated into a mere worship of the letter rather than the spirit.

IV
THE PLACE OF THE OLD TESTAMENT IN DIVINE REVELATION

Modern discovery and research have demonstrated that the truth revealed through the Babylonians and with less definiteness through the people of the Nile was never entirely lost. Such a sad waste was out of accord with the obvious principles of divine economy. As the icy chill of ceremonialism seized decadent Babylonia and Egypt, there emerged from the steppes south and east of Palestine a virile, ambitious group of nomads, who not only fell heir to that which was best in the revelation of the past, but also quickly took their place as the real spiritual leaders of the human race. Possibly their ancestors, like those of Hammurabi, belonged to that wave of nomadic emigration which swept out of overpopulated northern Arabia about 2500 B.C., part of it to settle finally in Babylonia and part in Palestine.

Whatever be the exact date of their advent, the much mooted and more fundamental question at once presents itself, Why were the Hebrews "the chosen people"? It is safe to assert at once that this was not arbitrary nor without reason. Moreover, the choice was not that of a moment, but gradual. Rather the real question is, By what divine process were the Israelites prepared to be the chosen people that their later prophets and the event of history declare them to be? Certain definite historical reasons at once suggest themselves; and these in turn throw new light upon the true relation of the Old Testament to divine revelation as a whole.

There is undoubtedly a basis for what Renan was pleased to call, "the Semitic genius for religion." It is a truly significant fact that the three great conquering religions of the world, Judaism, Christianity, and Mohammedanism, sprang from Semitic soil. To this might be added the religion of Babylonia, which, was unquestionably the noblest of early antiquity. In general the Semitic mind is keen, alert, receptive, and intuitional rather than logical. Restless energy and the tendency to acquire have also tended to make them leaders in the widely different fields of commerce and religion. The patriarch Jacob is a remarkable example of these combined qualities and results. By day he got the better of his kinsmen, and by night he wrestled with God. These combined and highly developed characteristics of mind and nature at least suggest why the Semites have furnished the greatest prophets and prophet nations for the moulding of the faith of the world.

In contrast with contemporary Semitic nations, and especially the highly civilized Babylonians, the Hebrews were fortunate in their immediate inheritances through Arabian or Aramean ancestors. The wandering, nomadic life leaves no place for established sanctuaries, with their elaborate ceremonial customs and debasing institutions inherited from more primitive ages. Instead, that life imposes limitations that make for simplicity. The mysteries and constant dangers of the wild desert existence also emphasize the constant necessity of divine help. The long marches by night under the silent stars inspire awe and enforce contemplation. The close unity of the tribe suggests the worship of one tribal god rather than many. From the desert the ancestors of the Hebrews brought strong bodies, inured to hardship, and a grim austerity that found frequent expression on the lips of their prophets and a response in the minds of the people, when luxury threatened to engulf them. They also inherited from their desert days those democratic ideas and high ideals of individual liberty which, enabled Elijah and Isaiah to stand up add champion the rights of the people even though it involved a public denunciation of their kings.

On the other hand, the Israelites undoubtedly became in time the inheritors of the best in religion and law that had been attained by the older Semitic races. Their late traditions trace back their ancestry to ancient Babylonia. Already for long centuries, by conquest and by commerce, the dominant civilization of the Euphrates valley had been regnant in the land of Canaan, The Tell-el-Amarna letters, written from Palestine in the fourteenth century, employ the Babylonian language and system of writing, and reveal a high Semitic civilization, closely patterned after that of Babylonia. When the Israelites settled in Canaan and began to intermarry and assimilate with the older inhabitants, as the earliest Hebrew records plainly state (cf. Judg. I.), they found there, among the Canaanites, established civil and religious institutions and traditions which were largely a reflection of those of Babylonia. Also, when in the eighth and seventh centuries

Assyrian armies conquered Palestine, they brought Babylonian institutions, traditions, and religious ideas. We know that during the reigns of Ahaz and Manasseh these threatened to displace those peculiar to the Hebrews. Again, during the Babylonian exile the influence of the same powerful civilization upon the thought and religion of Israel was also strongly felt. Thus the opportunities, direct and indirect, for receiving from Babylonia much of the rich heritage that it held were many and varied.

Certain parts of the Old Testament itself testify that the wealth of tradition, of institutions, of laws, and religious ideas, gradually committed to the Semitic ancestors of the Hebrews and best preserved by the Babylonians, was not lost, but, enriched and purified, has been transmitted to us through its pages. A careful comparison of the biblical and Babylonian accounts of the creation and the flood leaves little doubt that there is a close historical connection between these accounts. Investigation reveals in language, spirit, and form many analogies between the laws of Hammurabi and those of the Old Testament which suggest at least an indirect influence. Many of the ceremonial institutions of later Judaism are almost identical with those of Babylonia. While it is exceedingly easy to over or under estimate this influence, it is a mistake to deny or ignore its deep significance.

Thus one of the chief elements in the providential training of the Hebrews as the heralds and exponents of the most exalted religious and ethical truths revealed before the advent of the Prophet of Nazareth was the fact that they were the heirs and interpreters of the best that had been hitherto attained. Babylonia, Egypt, and later, Persia and Greece, each contributed their noblest beliefs and ideals. In the Israelites the diverse streams of divine revelation converged. The result is that, instead of many little rivulets, befouled by errors and superstitions, through their history there flowed a mighty stream, ever becoming broader and deeper and clearer as it received fresh contributions from the new fountains of purest revelation that opened in Hebrew soil.

Clear evidences of the divine purpose to be realized through the obscure peasant people who lived among the uplands of central Canaan are found in a study of the characteristics of the Old Testament world. It is indeed the earliest and one of the most significant chapters in divine revelation. Most of its area is a barren wilderness, supporting only a small nomadic population. The three fertile spots are Babylonia, Canaan, and Egypt. The first and last are fitted by nature and situation to be the seats of powerful civilizations, destined to reach out in every direction. Canaan, on the contrary, is shut in, with no good harbors along the Mediterranean; and its largest river system leads to the Dead Sea, far below the surface of the ocean, — an effective negation to all commerce. Although thus shut in by itself, Canaan lies on the isthmus of fertile land that connects the great empires of the Nile and the Euphrates. On the east and south it is always subject to the influences and waves of immigration, that come from the Arabian desert. It attracted from their nomadic life the ancestors of the Israelites, and during their early period of development gave them a secluded home. When they were ready to learn the larger lessons in the stream of life, Egypt and the great empires of the Tigris and Euphrates valley contended for them, conquered and ultimately scattered them throughout the then known world. While their conquerors, Egypt, Assyria, Babylonia, Persia, Greece, and Rome, the greatest powers of the ancient world, took from them their gold and their freedom, from the same conquerors they appear to have received the infinitely more precious treasures of tradition and thought.

Great as was their heritage from the past, the truth that came through the Hebrews themselves constitutes by far the greatest and most significant part of that revelation which the Old Testament records. Their history suggests the ways in which, Jehovah opened the spiritual eyes of the people. From the beginning to the present day it has been characterized by a series of crises unparalleled in the life of any other race. Experiences, intense and often superlatively painful, have come to them in rapid succession, forcing them to think and develop. The little street Arab, alert, resourceful, uncanny in his prematurity, is a modern illustration of what grim necessity and experience can produce. It was in the school supremely adapted to divine ends that Jehovah, trained his people to be his spokesmen to the world.

Other peoples, however, had their crises and yet had no such message as did the Israelites. What made the crises in the history of the Israelites richly fruitful in ethical and spiritual truth was the presence within their midst of certain devoted, responsive teachers, and especially the prophets, who guided them in their time of peril, interpreted its significance, and appealed to the awakened conscience of the nation. Like begets like. At the beginning of Israel's history stands the great prophet Moses, and during the long centuries that followed the voice of the prophets was rarely hushed.

In seeking the ultimate answer to our question, How were the Israelites prepared to be the chosen people, we are confronted by a miracle that baffles our power to analyze: it is the supreme fact that the Spirit of the Almighty touched the spirit of certain men in ancient Israel so that they became seers and prophets. This is their own testimony, and their deeds and words amply confirm it. The experiences of men to-day also demonstrate its possibility. Indeed it is not surprising, but most natural, that the one supreme Personality in the universe should reveal himself to and through human minds, and that the most enlightened men of the most spiritually enlightened race should be the recipients of the fullest and most perfect revelation. It is the truth that they thus perceived, and then proclaimed by word and deed and pen, that completed the preparation of the chosen people, for it was none other than the possession of a unique spiritual message that constituted the essence of their choice. Furthermore, as the greatest of the later prophets declares (Is. xl.-lv.), that divine choice did not mean that they were to be the recipients of exceptional favors, but rather that they were called to service. By the patient enduring of suffering and by voluntary self-sacrifice they were to perfect the revelation of God's character and will in the life of humanity.

The Old Testament, therefore, is the final record of a revelation extending through thousands of years, finding at last its most exalted expression in the messages of the Hebrew prophets, and its clearest reflection in the thoughts and experiences of the priests, sages, and psalmists of ancient Israel. In varied literary forms and by many different writers the best fruits of that revelation have been preserved. Ancient traditions, songs, proverbs, laws, historical narratives, prophecies, and psalms, each present their precious truth. The Israelitish race, however, never fully completed the work to which it was called. A master was needed to distinguish between the essential and the non-essential, to simplify and unify the teachings of the Old Testament as a whole, and to apply them personally to individual life, A man was demanded to realize fully in his own character the highest ideals of this ancient revelation. A divinely gifted prophet was required to perfect man's knowledge, and to bring him into natural, harmonious relations with his Eternal Father. The world awaited the advent of a Messiah who would establish, on the everlasting foundations of justice and truth and love, the universal kingdom of God. These supreme needs were met in fullest measure by the Master, the perfect Man, the Prophet, and the Messiah, whose work the New Testament records.

While there are many superficial points of difference in language, literary form, background, and point of view between the Old and the New Testaments, these are insignificant in comparison with the essential points of likeness and contact. Each Testament is but a different chapter in the history of the same divine revelation. The one is the foundation on which the other is built. The writers of the New constantly assume the historical facts, the institutions, and the teachings of the Old. Although in Greek garb, their language and idioms are also those of the Old. On many themes, as, for example, man's duty to society, Jesus said little, for the teachers of his race had fully developed them and there was little to add. Repeatedly by word and act he declared that he came not to destroy the older teachings, but simply to bring them to full perfection. The Old Testament also tells of the long years of preparation and of the earnest expectations of the Israelitish race; the New records a fulfilment far transcending the most exalted hopes of Hebrew seers. The same God reveals himself through both Testaments. One progressively unfolding system of religious teachings, one message of love, and one divine purpose bind both together with bonds that no generation or church can break.

V

THE INFLUENCES THAT PRODUCED THE NEW TESTAMENT

The present age is supremely interested in origins. Not until we have traced the genesis and earliest unfolding of an institution or an idea or a literature do we feel that we really understand and appreciate it. Familiarity with that which is noble breeds not contempt but reverence, and intelligent devotion. Acquaintance with the origin and history of a book is essential to its true interpretation. Therefore it is fortunate that modern discovery and research have thrown so much light upon the origin of both the Old and the New Testaments.

Equally fortunate is it that we are also learning to appreciate the sublimity and divinity of the natural. The universe and organic life are no less wonderful and awe-inspiring because, distinguishing some of the natural laws that govern their evolution, we have abandoned the grotesque theories held by primitive men. Similarly we do not to-day demand, as did our forefathers, a supernatural origin for our sacred books before we are ready to revere and obey their commands. With greater insight we now can heartily sing, "God moves in a natural way his wonders to perform." Our ability to trace the historical influences through which he brought into being and shaped the two Testaments and gave them their present position in the life of humanity does not in a thoughtful mind obscure, but rather reveals the more clearly, their divine origin and authority.

Through contemporary writings and the results of modern biblical research it is possible to study definitely the origin of the various New Testament books and to follow the different stages in their growth into a canon. This familiar chapter in the history of the Bible is richly suggestive, because of the clear light which it sheds upon the more complex and obscure genesis and later development of the Old Testament. It will be profitable, therefore, to review it in outline, not only because of its own importance, but also as an introduction to the study of the influences that produced the older Scriptures; for almost every fact that will be noted in connection with the origin and literary history of the New has its close analogy in the growth of the Old Testament.

We find that as they are at present arranged, the books of the New Testament are divided into three distinct classes. The first group includes the historical books: the Gospels and Acts; the second, the Epistles — the longer, like the letters to the Romans and Corinthians, being placed first and the shorter at the end; while the third group contains but one book, known as the Apocalypse or Revelation. The general arrangement is clearly according to subject-matter, not according to date of authorship; the order of the groups represent different stages in the process of canonization.

Their position as well as the themes which they treat suggest that the Gospels were the first to be written. It is, however, a self-evident fact that a book was not written — at least not in antiquity, when the making of books was both laborious and expensive — unless a real need for it was felt. If we go back, and live for a moment in imagination among the band of followers which Jesus left behind at his death, we see clearly that while the early Christian Church was limited to Palestine, and a large company of disciples, who had often themselves seen and heard the Christ, lived to tell by word of mouth the story of his life and teachings, no one desired a written record. It is not surprising, therefore, that the oldest books in the New Testament are not the Gospels. The exigencies of time and space and the burning zeal of the apostles for the churches of their planting apparently produced the earliest Christian writings.

In his second missionary journey Paul preached for a time at Thessalonica, winning to faith in the Christ a small mixed company of Jews and proselyte Greeks. His success aroused the bitter opposition of the narrower Jews, who raised a mob and drove him from the city before his work was completed. But the seed which he had planted continued to grow. Naturally he was eager to return to the infant church. Twice he planned to visit it, but was prevented. In his intense desire to help the brave Christians of Thessalonica, he sent Timothy to inquire regarding their welfare and to encourage them. When about 50 A.D. Timothy reported to Paul at Corinth, the apostle wrote at once to the little church at Thessalonica a letter of commendation, encouragement, and counsel, which we know to-day as

First Thessalonians and which is probably one of the oldest writings in our New Testament, Galatians perhaps being the earliest.

Another letter (II Thess.) soon followed, giving more detailed advice. As the field of Paul's activity broadened, he was obliged more and more to depend upon letters, since he could not in person visit the churches which he had planted. Questions of doctrine as well as of practice which perplexed the different churches were treated in these epistles. To certain of his assistants, like Timothy, he wrote dealing with their personal problems. Frankly, forcibly, and feelingly Paul poured out in these letters the wealth of his personal and soul life. They reveal his faith in the making as well as his mature teachings. Since he was dealing with definite conditions in the communities to which he wrote, his letters are also invaluable contemporary records of the growth and history of the early Christian church. Thus between 30 and 60 A.D., during the period of his greatest activity, certainly ten, and probably thirteen, of our twenty-seven New Testament books came from the burning heart of the apostle to the Gentiles.

Similar needs impelled other apostles and early Christian teachers to write on the same themes with the same immediate purpose as did Paul. The result is a series of epistles, associated with the names of James, Peter, John, and Jude. In some, like Third John, the personal element is predominant; in others, the didactic, as, for example, the Epistle of James.

A somewhat different type of literature is represented by the Epistle to the Hebrews. Its form is that of a letter, and it was without doubt originally addressed to a local church or churches by a writer whose name has ever since been a fertile source of conjecture. The only fact definitely established is that Paul did not write it. It is essentially a combination of argument, doctrine, and exhortation. The aim is apologetic as well as practical. Most of Paul's letters were written as the thoughts, which he wished to communicate to those to whom he wrote, came to his mind; but in the Epistle to the Hebrews the author evidently follows a carefully elaborated plan. The argument is cumulative. The thesis is that Christ, superior to all earlier teachers of his race, is the perfect Mediator of Salvation.

Thus the Epistles, originally personal notes of encouragement and warning, growing sometimes into more elaborate treatises, were made the means whereby the early Christian teachers imparted their doctrines to constantly widening groups of readers. At best they were regarded simply as inferior substitutes for the personal presence and spoken words of their authors. Like the Old Testament books, their authority lies in the fact that they faithfully reflect, in part at least, the greater revelation coming through the lives and minds of the early apostles.

As is well known, the twenty-one letters in our New Testament were selected from a far larger collection of epistles, some of which were early lost, while others, like the Epistles of Barnabas and Polycarp and Clement, were preserved to share with those later accepted as canonical, the study and veneration of the primitive Church.

The influences which originally produced the Gospels and Acts were very different from those which called forth the Epistles. The natural preference of the early Christians for the spoken word explains why we do not possess to-day a single written sentence in the Gospels which we can with absolute assurance assign to the first quarter-century following the death of Jesus. Two influences, however, in time led certain writers to record his early life and teachings. The one was that death was rapidly thinning the ranks of those who could say, I saw and heard; the other was the spread of Christianity beyond the bounds of Judaism and Palestine, and the resulting need for detailed records felt by those Christians who had never visited Palestine and who had learned from the lips of apostles only the barest facts regarding the life of the Christ.

The opening verses of Luke's Gospel are richly suggestive of the origin and growth of the historical books of the New Testament:

Forasmuch as many have taken in hand to draw up a narrative concerning those matters which have been fulfilled among us, even as they delivered them unto us, — they who from the beginning were eye-witnesses and ministers of the word, it seemed good to me also, having traced the course of all things accurately from the first, to write unto thee in order, most excellent Theophilus, that thou mightest know the certainty concerning the things wherein thou wast instructed.

This prologue states that many shorter Gospels had previously been written, not by eye-witnesses, but by men who had listened to those who had themselves seen. Luke leaves his readers to infer that he also drew a large number of his facts from these earlier sources as well as from the testimony of eye-witnesses. The implication of the prologue is that he himself was entirely dependent upon written and oral sources for his data. This is confirmed by the testimony of the Muratorian Fragment:

Luke the physician, after the ascension of Christ, when Paul had taken him, as it were, as a follower zealous of the right, wrote the gospel book according to Luke in his own name, as is believed. Nevertheless he had not himself seen the Lord in the flesh, and, accordingly, going back as far as he could obtain information, he began his narrative with the birth of John.

His many literal quotations from it and the fact that he makes it the framework of his own, indicate that Mark's Gospel was one of those earlier attempts to which he refers.

The motive which influenced Luke to write is clearly stated. It was to prepare a comprehensive, accurate, and orderly account of the facts in regard to the life of Jesus for his Greek friend Theophilus, who had already been partially instructed in the same. His Gospel confirms the implications of the prologue. It is the longest and most carefully arranged of all the Gospels. The distinctively Jewish ideas or institutions which are prominent in Matthew are omitted or else explained; hence there is nothing which would prove unintelligible to a Greek. The book of the Acts of the Apostles, dedicated to the same patron, is virtually a continuation of the third Gospel, tracing, in a more or less fragmentary manner, the history and growth, of the early Christian Church, and especially the work of Paul.

Very similar influences called forth the shortest and undoubtedly the oldest of the four Gospels, the book of Mark. The testimony of the contents confirms in general the early statement of Papias and other Christian Fathers that it was written at Rome by John Mark, the disciple and interpreter of the apostle Peter, after the death of his teacher. The absence of many Old Testament quotations, the careful explanation of all Jewish and Palestinian references which would not be intelligible to a foreigner, the presence of certain Latin words, and many other indications, all tend to establish the conclusion that it was written for the Gentile and Jewish Christians, probably at Rome, and that its purpose was simply historical.

The memoir of Jesus, which we know as the Gospel of Matthew, is from the hand of a Jewish Christian and, as is shown by the amount of material drawn from Mark's Gospel, must be placed at a later date. The great number of quotations from the Old Testament, the interest in tracing the fulfilment of the Messianic predictions, and the distinctively Jewish-Christian point of view and method of interpretation, indicate clearly that he wrote not with Gentile but Jewish Christians in mind. Nevertheless, like that of Mark and Luke, his purpose was primarily to present a faithful and, as far as his sources permitted, detailed picture of the life and teachings of Jesus. His arrangement of his material appears, however, to be logical rather than purely chronological. The different sections and the individual incidents and teachings each contribute to the great argument of the book, namely, that Jesus was the true Messiah of the Jews; that the Jews, since they rejected him, forfeited their birthright; and that his kingdom, fulfilling and inheriting the Old Testament promises, has become a universal kingdom, open to all races and freed from all Jewish bonds. Cf. e.g., x. 5, 6; xv. 24; viii. 11, 12; xii. 38-45; xxi. 42, 43; xxii. 7; xxiii. 13, 36, 38; xxiv. 2; xxviii. 19 This suggests that the First Gospel represents a more mature stage in the thought of the early Church than Mark and Luke.

Its title and the fact that the Church Fathers constantly connect it with Matthew, the publican, and later apostle is explained by the statement of Papias, quoted by Eusebius:

Matthew accordingly composed the oracles in the Hebrew dialect, and each one interpreted them as he was able (H.E., iii. 39). These oracles evidently consisted of a written collection of the sayings of Jesus. Since they were largely if not entirely included in our First Gospel, It was therefore known as The Gospel of Matthew. There is no evidence that the original

Matthew's Sayings of Jesus contained definite narrative material. The fact that the First Gospel draws so largely from Mark for its historical data would indicate that this was not supplied by its main source. The Sayings of Jesus was probably the oldest written record of the work of Jesus, for, while oral tradition, easily remembers incidents, disconnected teachings are not so readily preserved by the memory. Their transcendent importance would also furnish a strong incentive to use the pen. It was natural also that, of all the disciples, the ex-customs officer of Capernaum should be the one to undertake this transcendently important task.

The Fourth is clearly the latest of the Gospels, for it does not attempt fully to reproduce the facts presented in the other three, but assumes their existence. Its doctrines are also more fully developed, and its aim is not simply the giving of historical facts and teachings, but also, as it clearly states, that those reading it might believe that Jesus was the Christ, the son of God, and that believing they might have life in his name (xx. 31). The motive that produced it was, therefore, apologetic and evangelical rather than merely historical.

A detailed comparison of the differences between the Gospels, as well as of their many points of likeness which often extend to exact verbal agreement, furnishes the data for reconstructing their history. In general the resulting conclusions are in perfect harmony with the testimony of the Church Fathers. Mark, the shortest and more distinctively narrative Gospel, is clearly the oldest of the four. Possibly it was originally intended to be the supplement of the other early source, Matthew's Sayings of Jesus, now known only through quotations. These two earliest known Christian records of the work of the Master in their original form were the chief sources quoted in the First and Third Gospels. So largely is Mark thus reproduced that, if lost, it would be possible from these to restore the book with the exception of only a few verses. But in addition, Matthew and Luke each have material peculiar to themselves, suggesting other independent written as well as oral sources. To such shorter written Gospels, and also to the oral testimony of eyewitnesses, Luke refers in his prologue. In the Fourth Gospel, the doctrinal motive already apparent in Matthew, and prominent in the Church at the beginning of the second Christian century, takes the precedence of the merely historical. A distinct source, the personal observation of the beloved disciple, probably also furnishes the majority of the illustrations which are here so effectively arrayed.

More complex were the influences which produced the single example of the third type of New Testament literature, — the Apocalypse, or Book of Revelation. The so-called apocalyptic type of literature was a characteristic product of later Judaism. The Book of Daniel is the most familiar example. Although in the age of scribism the voice of the prophets was regarded as silent, and the only authority recognized was that of the past, the popular Messianic hopes of the people continued to find expression anonymously in the form of apocalypses. In the periods of their greatest distress Jews and Christians found encouragement and inspiration in the pictures of the future. Since the present situation was so hopeless, they looked for a supernatural transformation, which would result in the triumph of the right and the establishment of the rule of the Messiah. Underlying all the apocalypses is the eternal truth voiced by the poet: "God's in his heaven and all's right with the world."

The immediate historical background of the Apocalypse is the bitter struggle between Christianity and heathenism. Rome has become drunk with the blood of the saints and the blood of the martyrs of Jesus (xvii. 6). The contest centres about the worship of the beast, — that is, Caesar. The book possibly includes older apocalypses which reflect earlier conflicts, but in its present form it apparently comes from the closing years of Domitian's reign. The obvious aim of its Jewish Christian writer was to encourage his readers by glowing pictures of the coming victory of the Lamb, and thus to steel them for unfaltering resistance to the assaults of heathenism. The purpose which actuated the writer was therefore in certain respects the same as that which led Paul to write his letter to the persecuted church of Thessalonica, although the form in which that purpose was realized was fundamentally different.

Many other apocalypses were written by the early Christians. The one recently discovered and associated with the name of Peter is perhaps the most important. Thus, the second half of the first century after the death of Jesus witnessed the birth of a large Christian literature, consisting of epistles, gospels, and apocalypses. The work of the next three centuries was the appreciation and the selection of the books which, to-day constitute our New Testament. The influences which led to this consummation may be followed almost as clearly as those which produced the individual books.

Early in the second century the motives which had originally led certain Christians to write the four Gospels induced the Church to regard those books as the most authentic, and therefore authoritative, records of the life and teachings of the Master. We have no distinctive history of the process. It was gradual, and probably almost unconscious. The fact that three of the Gospels were associated with the names of apostles and the other with Luke, the faithful companion of Paul, undoubtedly tended to establish their authority; but the chief canonizing influence was the need of such records for private and public reading. The production, early in the second century, of spurious gospels, like the Gospel of Marcion, written to furnish a literary basis for certain heretical doctrines, also the desire of the Church Fathers to have records to which they could appeal as authoritative hastened the formation of the first New Testament canon. The use of the Gospels in the services of the church, which probably began before the close of the first Christian century, by degrees gave them an authority equal to that of the Old Testament Scriptures. The earliest canon consisted simply of these four books. They seem to have been universally accepted by the Western Church by the middle of the second century. About 152 A.D. Justin Martyr, in proving his positions, refers to the Memoirs of the Apostles compiled by Christ's apostles and those who associated with them, and during the same decade his pupil Tatian made his Diatessaron by combining our present four Gospels.

Meantime the natural desire to supplement the teachings of Jesus by those of the Apostles led the Church to single out certain of the epistles and associate them with the Gospels. Already in the first century the apostolic epistles and traditions were cherished by the individual churches to which they had been first directed. In time, however, the need for a written record of the apostolic teachings and work became widely felt. Hence, by the end of the second century, Acts and the thirteen Pauline epistles, First Peter, First John, and the Apocalypse, were by common consent placed side by side with the Gospels, at least by the leaders of the Western Church.

Regarding the authority of the remaining New Testament books, Hebrews, James, First and Second John, and Jude, opinion long remained undecided. Concerning them an earnest discussion was carried on for the next two centuries. By certain leaders in the Church they were regarded as authoritative, while elsewhere and at different periods, other books, like the Gospel to the Hebrews, the Epistle of Barnabas, Clement's Epistle to the Corinthians, the Shepherd of Hermas, and the Apocalypse of Peter, were included in the canon and even given the priority over the disputed books later included in our New Testament.

The final decision represents the result of an open and prolonged and yet quiet consideration of the merits of each book and of its claims to apostolic authority. The ablest scholars of the early Christian Church devoted their best energies to the problem. Gradually, thoughtfully, prayerfully, and by testing them in the laboratory of experience, the Christian world separated the twenty-seven books which we find to-day in our New Testament from the much larger heritage of kindred writings which come from the early Christian centuries. Time and later consideration have fully approved the selection and confirmed the belief that through the minds of consecrated men God was realizing his purpose for mankind. As is well known, at the Council of Carthage, in 397 A.D., the Western world at last formally accepted them, although the Syrian churches continued for centuries to retain a somewhat different canon.

This brief historical study of the origin of our New Testament has demonstrated twelve significant facts: (1) That the original authors of the different books never suspected that their writings would have the universal value and authority which they now rightfully enjoy. (2) That they at first regarded them as merely an imperfect substitute for verbal teaching and personal testimony. (3) That in each case they had definite individuals and conditions in mind. (4) That the needs of the rapidly growing Church and the varied and trying experiences through which it passed were all potent factors in influencing the authors of the New Testament to write. (5) That certain books, especially the historical, like Luke and Matthew, are composite, consisting of material taken bodily from older documents, like Matthew's Sayings of Jesus and the original narrative of Mark. (6) That our New Testament books are only a part of a much larger early Christian literature. (7) That they are unquestionably, however, the most valuable and representative writings of that larger literature. (8) That they were only gradually selected and ascribed a value and authority equal to that of the Old Testament writings. (9) That there were three distinct stages in the formation of the New Testament canon: the gospels were first recognized as authorative; then Acts, the Apostolic Epistles, and the Apocalypse; and last of all, the complete canon. (10) That the canon was formed as a result of the need felt by later generations, in connection with their study and worship, for reliable records of the history and teachings of Christianity. (11) That the principles of selection depended ultimately upon the intrinsic character of the books themselves and the authority ascribed to their reputed authors. (12) That the process of selection continued for fully three centuries, and that the results represent the thoughtful, enlightened judgment of thousands of devoted Christians. Thus through definite historical forces and the minds and wills of men, the Eternal Father gradually perfected the record of his supreme revelation, to humanity.

VI

THE GROWTH OF THE OLD TESTAMENT PROPHETIC HISTORIES

Very similar influences were at work in producing and shaping both the Old and the New Testaments; only in the history of the older Scriptures still other forces can be distinguished. Moreover, the Old Testament contains a much greater variety of literature. It is also significant that, while some of the New Testament books began to be canonized less than a century after they were written, there is clear evidence that many of the Old Testament writings were in existence several centuries before they were gathered together into a canon and thus crystallized into their final form. The inevitable result is that they bear the marks of much more elaborate editorial revision than those of the New. It is, however, not the aim of the present work to trace this complex process of revision in detail, nor to give the cumulative evidence and the many data and reasons that lead to each conclusion. These can be studied in any modern Old Testament introduction or in the volumes of the present writer's Student's Old Testament.

In their present form, the books of the Old Testament, like those of the New, fall into three classes. The first includes the historical books. In the Old, corresponding to the four Gospels and Acts of the New, are found the books from Genesis through Esther. Next in order, in the Old, stand the poetical books, from Job through the Song of Songs, with which the New Testament has no analogy except the liturgical hymns connected with the nativity, preserved in the opening chapters of Matthew and Luke. The third group in the Old Testament includes the prophecies from Isaiah through Malachi.

One book in this group, Daniel, and portions of Ezekiel and Joel, are analogous to the New Testament Apocalypse, but otherwise the prophetic books correspond closely in character and contents to the epistles of the New. Both are direct messages to contemporaries of the prophets and apostles, and both deal with then existing conditions. Both consist of practical warnings, exhortations, advice, and encouragement. The form is simply incidental. The prophets of Jehovah preached, and then they or their disciples wrote down the words which they had addressed to their countrymen. When they could not reach with their voices all in whom they were interested, the prophets, like the apostles, committed their teachings to writing and sent them forth as tracts (cf. Jer. xxxvi.). At other times, when they could not go in person, they wrote letters. Thus, for example, the twenty-ninth chapter of the prophecy of Jeremiah opens with the interesting superscription:

Now these are the words of the letter that Jeremiah the prophet sent from Jerusalem unto the residue of the elders of the captivity, and to the priests, and to the prophets, and to all the people, whom Nebuchadrezzar had carried away captive from Jerusalem to Babylon; by the hand of Elasah the son of Shaphan, and Gemariah the son of Hilkiah, whom Zedekiah king of Judah sent unto Babylon to Nebuchadrezzar.

If it were not for this superscription, no one would suspect from the nature of the letter which follows that it was anything other than a regular spoken or written prophecy. Its contents and spirit are exactly parallel to those of Paul's epistles. Undoubtedly many prophecies were never delivered orally, but were originally written like Paul's Epistle to the Ephesians, and sent out as circular letters. The Babylonian exile scattered the Jews so widely that the exilic and post-exilic prophets depended almost entirely upon this method of reaching their countrymen and thus became writers of epistles.

Like the Epistles in the New, certain of the prophecies,—as, for example, those of Amos, Hosea, and Isaiah,—are among the earliest writings of the Old Testament. But in the light of modern biblical study, it has become apparent that prose was not the earliest form of expression among the Hebrews, In this respect their literary history is parallel with that of other early peoples; for first they treasured their thought in heroic song and ballad. While they were nomads, wandering in the desert, and also while they were struggling for the possession of Canaan, they had little time or motive for cultivating the literary art. The popular songs which were sung beside the camp-fires, at the recurring festivals, and as the Hebrews advanced in battle against their foes, were the earliest records of their past. There is evidence that many of the primitive narratives now found in the opening chapters of Genesis were also once current in poetical form. In some cases the poetic structure has been preserved.

The earliest collections of writings referred to in the Old Testament bear the suggestive titles, The Book of the Upright (i.e., Israel), and, The Book of the Wars of Jehovah. From the quotations which we have from them it is clear that they consisted of collections of songs, recounting the exploits of Israel's heroes and the signal victories of the race.

That stirring paean of victory known as the Song of Deborah was perhaps once found in the Book of the Wars of Jehovah. It is one of the oldest pieces of literature in the Old Testament, and breathes the heroic spirit of the primitive age from which it comes. Through the eyes of the poet one views the different scenes in the mighty conflict. The translation is from "The Student's Old Testament," Vol. I., pp. 320-323.

That the leaders took the lead in Israel,

That the people volunteered readily,

Bless Jehovah!

Hear, O kings,

Give ear, O rulers.

I myself will sing to Jehovah,

I will sing praise to Jehovah, the God of Israel.

Jehovah, when thou wentest forth from Seir,

When thou marchest from the land of Edom,

The earth trembled, the heavens also dripped,

Yea, the clouds dropped water.

The mountains quaked before Jehovah,

Yon Sinai before Jehovah, the God of Israel.

In the days of Shamgar the son of Anath,

In the days of Jael, the highways ceased to be used,

And travellers walked by round-about paths.

The rulers ceased in Israel, they ceased,

Until than didst arise, Deborah,

Until thou didst arise a mother in Israel.

Then the people of Jehovah went down to the gates, crying,

"Arise, arise, Deborah,

Arise, arise, strike up the song!

Arise Barak, and take thy captives, thou son of Abinoam!"

So a remnant went down against the powerful,

The people of Jehovah went down against the mighty,

From Ephraim they rushed forth into the valley,

Thy brother Benjamin among thy peoples,

From Machir went down, commanders,

And from Zebulun those who carry the marshal's staff.

And the princes of Issachar were with Deborah;

And Napthali was even so with Barak,

Into the valley they rushed forth at his back.

By the brooks of Reuben great were the resolves!

Why didst they sit among the sheepfolds,

Listening to the pipings for the flocks?

By the brooks of Reuben there were great questionings!

Gilead remained beyond the Jordan;

And Dan, why does he stay by the ships as an alien?

Asher sits still by the shore of the sea,

And remains by its landings.

Zebulun was a people who exposed their lives to deadly peril,

And Napthali on the heights of the open field.

Bless Jehovah!

Kings came, they fought;

Then fought the kings of Canaan,

At Taanach by the waters of Megiddo;

They took no booty of silver.

From heaven fought the stars,

From their courses fought against Sisera.

The river Kishon swept them away,

The ancient river, the river Kishon.

O my soul, march on with strength!

Then did the horse-hoofs resound

With the galloping, galloping of the powerful steeds.

In the Book of the Upright is included that
touching elegy which David sang after the
death of Saul and Jonathan, and which stands
next to the Song of Deborah as one of the
earliest surviving examples of Old Testament
literature.

Weep, O Judah!

Grieve, O Israel!

On thy heights are the slain!

How have the mighty fallen!

Tell it not in Gath,

Declare it not in the streets of Askelon;

Lest the daughters of the Philistines rejoice,

Lest the daughters of the uncircumcised exult.

Ye mountains of Gilboa, may no dew descend,

Nor rain upon you, O ye fields of death!

For there was the shield of the mighty cast away,

The shield of Saul, not anointed with oil.

From the blood of the slain,

From the fat of the mighty,

The bow of Jonathan turned not back,

The sword of Saul returned not empty.

Saul and Jonathan, the beloved and the lovely!

In life and in death they were not parted;

They were swifter than eagles,

They were stronger than lions.

Daughters of Israel, weep over Saul,

Who clothed you daintily in fine linen,

Who put golden ornaments on your garments, and say:

"How have the mighty fallen in the midst of battle!"

Jonathan, in thy death hast thou wounded me!

I am distressed for thee, my brother Jonathan!

Thou wert surpassingly dear to me,

Thy love to me was far more than the love of woman!

How have the mighty fallen,

And the weapons of war perished!

The so-called Blessing of Jacob (Gen. xlix, 2-27) is a poetical delineation of the strength and weakness of the different tribes of Israel with references to specific events in their history. These historical allusions suggest that it probably comes from the reigns of David and Solomon, when the tribes were for the first time all united under a common rule and had passed through certain of the experiences alluded to in the poem.

The Israelitish race was supremely rich in possessing not only many ancient songs, but also a large body of oral traditions which had long been handed down from father to son or else treasured by the story-tellers and by the priests of the ancient sanctuaries. Many of these traditions were inherited from their Semitic ancestors, and, in the light of recently discovered Babylonian literature, can be traced back far beyond the days of Abraham and Moses. Some were originally the possessions of certain nomadic tribes; others recorded the early experiences of their ancestors or told of the achievements of early heroes. In the process of continuous retelling, all unnecessary details had been eliminated and the really dramatic and essential elements emphasized, until they attained their present simple, graphic form, which fascinates young and old alike.

The superlative value of these varied traditions is apparent. They were the links which bound later generations to their prehistoric past. Incidentally, in the characteristic language of Semitic tradition, they preserved the memory of many important events in their early tribal history. They are also the illuminating record of the primitive beliefs, customs, and aspirations of their Semitic ancestors. Subject as they inevitably were to the idealizing tendency, they became in time the concrete embodiment of the noblest ideals of later generations. Thus they presented before the kindled imagination of each succeeding age, in the character and achievements of their traditional ancestors, those ideals of courage, perseverance, and piety which contributed much toward making the Israelites the chosen people that they were.

In time this growing heritage of traditions became too great for even the remarkable Oriental memory to retain. Meantime the Hebrews had also acquired that system of writing which they learned from their more civilized neighbors the Canaanites and Phoenicians. From, the days of Solomon, scribes were to be found in court and temple, and probably among the prophetic guilds; although the common people, as in the same land to-day, doubtless had little knowledge of the literary art. While the nation was struggling for the soil of Canaan, or enjoying the full tide of victory and achievement that came under the leadership of David, there was no time or incentive to write history. But with the quieter days of Solomon's reign, and the contrasting period of national decline that followed his death, the incentive to take up the pen and record the departed glories became strong. With a large body of definite oral traditions dealing with all the important men and events of the earlier periods, the task of the historian was chiefly that of writing down and coordinating what was already at hand.

The oldest Hebrew history that has been preserved in the Old Testament was the work of an unknown Judean prophet or group of prophets who lived and labored probably during the latter part of the ninth century before Christ. This history corresponds closely in relative age and aim to Mark's graphic narrative of the chief facts in the life of Jesus. The motive which influenced the earliest historians both of the Old and New Testaments to write was primarily the religious significance of the events which they thus recorded. This early Judean prophetic history (technically known as J) begins with the account of the creation of man from the dust by the hand of Jehovah, and tells of the first sin and its dire consequences (Gen. ii. 4 to iii. 24); then it gives an ancient list of those who stood as the fathers of nomads, of musicians and workers in metal (Gen. iv. 1, 16b-26). This is followed by the primitive stories of the sons of God and the daughters of men (Gen. vi. 1-4), of Noah the first vineyard-keeper (ix. 20-27), and of the tower of Babel and the origin of different languages (xi. 1-9). In a series of more or less closely connected narratives the character and experiences of the patriarchs, the life of the Hebrews in Egypt and the wilderness, and the settlement in Canaan are presented. Its basis for the history of the united kingdom was for the most part the wonderfully graphic group of Saul and David stories which occupy the bulk of the books of Samuel. Thus this remarkable early Judean prophetic history begins with the creation of the universe and man and concludes with the creation of the Hebrew empire.

In its present Old Testament form it has been closely combined with other histories, just as Mark's narrative is largely reproduced in Matthew and Luke; but when, it is separated from the later narratives its unity and completeness are astounding. Almost without a break it presents the chief characters and events of Israel's history in their relations to each other. The same peculiar vocabulary, the use of Jehovah as the designation of the Deity, the same vivid, flowing narrative style, the same simple, naïve, primitive conception of Jehovah, the same patriotic interest in the history of the race, and the same emphasis upon the vital religious significance of men and facts, characterize every section of this narrative and make comparatively easy the task of separating it from the other histories with which it has been joined.

A little later, sometime about the middle of the eighth century before Christ, a prophet or group of prophets in Northern Israel devoted themselves to the similar task of writing the history of Israel from the point of view of the northern kingdom. Since this state is called Ephraim by Hosea and other writers of the North, its history may be designated as the early Ephraimite prophetic (technically known as E). Naturally its author or authors utilized as the basis of their work the oral traditions current in the North. Sometimes these are closely parallel, and sometimes they vary widely in order and representation from the Judean versions. In general the variations are similar, although somewhat greater than those between the parallel narratives of Matthew and Luke.

Marked peculiarities in vocabulary and literary style distinguish this northern history from the Judean. Since Elohim or God is consistently used to describe the Deity, it has sometimes been called the Elohistic history. Interest inclines to the sanctuaries and heroes and events prominent in the life of the North. In that land which produced a Samuel, an Elijah, an Elisha, and an Hosea, it was natural that especial emphasis should be placed on the role of the prophet. Throughout these narratives he is portrayed as the dominant figure, moulding the history as God's representative. Abraham and Moses are here conceived of as prophets, and the Ephraimite history of their age is largely devoted to a portrayal of their prophetic activity.

The interests of later editors who combined these early prophetic histories, as we now find them in the Old Testament, were centred in the Judean, and hence they have introduced citations from the Ephraimite narratives chiefly to supplement the older history. Possibly it never was as complete as that of the South. At present it begins with Abraham and traces the parallel history of the patriarchs and the life of the Hebrews in Egypt and the wilderness. Its account of the conquest, is somewhat fuller, probably because Joshua was a northern leader. It also preserves many of the stories of the heroes in the book of Judges. With these the citations from the early Ephraimite prophetic history seem to disappear, but the opening stories in the book of Samuel, regarding the great prophet whose name was given to the book, apparently come from the pen of later disciples of this same Ephraimite group of prophets.

The eighth and seventh centuries before Christ were periods of intense prophetic activity both in the North and the South. It was natural, therefore, that these early prophetic histories should be supplemented by the disciples of the original historians. Traditions that possessed a permanent historical or religious value, as, for example, the familiar story of Cain and Abel (Gen. iv. 2-16), and the earlier of the two accounts of the flood, were thus added. Also when in 722 B.C. the northern kingdom fell and its literary heritage passed to Judah, it was most natural that a prophetic editor, recognizing the valuable elements in each, and the difficulties presented by the existence of the two variant versions of the same events, should combine the two, and furthermore that, in the days of few manuscripts, the older originals should be lost and only the combined history survive. To-day we find this in turn incorporated in the still later composite history extending from Genesis through Samuel.

The later editor's method of uniting his sources is exceedingly interesting, and is analogous in many ways to the methods followed in the citations in Matthew and Luke from their common sources, the original Mark and Matthew's Sayings of Jesus. Where the two versions were closely parallel, as in the account of Jacob's deception of his father Isaac, or the story of the spies, the two are completely amalgamated; short passages, verses, and parts of verses are taken in turn from each. In other cases the editor introduced the different versions — as, for example, the two accounts of the flight of Hagar — into different settings. From subsequent allusions to two versions, of which only one survives in the Old Testament, it is to be inferred that sometimes he simply preserved the fuller, usually the Judean. As a rule, however, there is clear evidence that he made every effort to retain all that he found in his original sources, even though the resulting composite narrative contained many inconsistencies.

Practical value of the rediscovery of the original histories

To the careful student, seeking to recover the original narratives in their primal unity, these inconsistencies are guides as valuable as the fossils and stratification of the earth are to the geologist intent upon tracing the earth's past history. Guided by these variations and the distinctive peculiarities in vocabulary, literary style, point of view, religious conceptions, and purpose of each of the groups of narratives, Old Testament scholars have rediscovered these two original histories; and with their recovery the great majority of seeming inconsistencies and many perplexing problems fade into insignificance. Supplementing each other, as do the earliest Gospels, these two independent histories present with new definiteness and authority the essential facts in Israel's early political, social and religious life. Like eye-witnesses, they testify to the still more significant fact that from the first God was revealing his character and will through a unique race.

A third survey of the period beginning with the sojourn in Egypt and concluding with the conquest of the east-Jordan land is found in the introduction to the book of Deuteronomy. It is the prologue to the laws that follow, appropriately and effectively placed in the mouth of the pioneer prophet Moses. A comparison quickly demonstrates that it is in reality a brief summary of the older histories, and especially of the early Ephraimite prophetic. Like the Gospel of Matthew, its aim is not merely to present historical facts, but to illustrate and establish a thesis. The thesis is that

Jehovah has personally led his people, and that when they have been faithful to him they have prospered, but when they have disobeyed calamity has overtaken, them. The message is distinctly prophetic; and to distinguish this third history, which was probably written near the close of the seventh century before Christ, from the earlier, it may be designated as the late prophetic or Deuteronomic history(technically represented by D).

These three prophetic histories correspond strikingly to the three synoptic Gospels: Mark, Luke and Matthew. The essential differences in their literary history are that they come, not from a single limited group of writers and a brief quarter century, but represent the work of many hands and at least two hundred and fifty years of literary activity. Two, at least, of these histories, are no longer extant in their original form, but only as they have been quoted verbatim by later historians and closely amalgamated. Similarly, as is well known, Tatian, the pupil of Justin Martyr, in the middle of the second Christian century, did for the four Gospels precisely what an Old Testament editor did for the two early prophetic histories, — he combined them into one composite, continuous narrative. By joining passages and verses and parts of verses taken from the different Gospels, by omitting verbal duplicates, by rearranging in some cases and by occasionally adding a word or phrase to join dissimilar parts, Tatian produced a marvellous mosaic gospel, known as the Diatessaron. All of the Fourth Gospel is thus preserved, and most of the first three. So successfully was the work done that the volume was widely used throughout the Eastern Church. If, as once seemed possible, it had completely supplanted the original four Gospels, the literary history of these would have been a repetition of that of the earliest Old Testament records.

It is very important to note that the motive which led the prophetic historians to commit to writing the earlier traditions of their race was not primarily historical. Like the author of the Fourth Gospel, they selected their material chiefly with a view to enforcing certain important religious truths. If an ancient Semitic tradition illustrated their point, they divested it of its heathen clothing and, irrespective of its origin, pressed it into service. For example, it seems clear that the elements which enter into the story of the Garden of Eden and man's fall were current, with variations, among the ancient Babylonians centuries before the Hebrews inherited them from their Semitic ancestors. The early prophet who wrote the second and third chapters of Genesis appreciated their value as illustrations, and made them the medium for imparting some of the most important spiritual truths ever conveyed to mankind. Like the preachers or moral teachers of to-day, the first question the prophets asked about a popular story was not, Is it absolutely historical or scientifically exact? but, Does it illustrate the vital point to be impressed? Undoubtedly Israel's heritage of oral traditions was far greater than is suggested by the narratives of the Old Testament; but only those which individually and collectively enforced some important religious truth, were utilized. Just as Jesus drew his illustrations from nature and human life about him, so these earlier spiritual teachers, with equal tact, took their illustrations from the familiar atmosphere of song and story and national tradition in which their readers lived. A secondary purpose, which they obviously had in view, was also to remove from certain of the popular tales the immoral implications which still clung to them from their heathen past, and to reconsecrate them to a diviner end.

Questions of relative date and historical accuracy concern the historian, but they should not obscure the greater value of these narratives. To the majority of us, who turn to the Old Testament simply as the record of divine revelation and as a guide to life, the essential thing is to put ourselves into touch with these ancient prophets, who taught by illustration as well as by direct address, and ask, What was the ethical or spiritual truth that illumined their souls and finds concrete expression and illustration through these primitive stories? To discuss the literal historicity of the story of the Garden of Eden is as absurd as to seek to discover who was the sower who went forth to sow or the Samaritan who went down to Jericho. Even, if no member of the despised Samaritan race ever followed in the footsteps of an hypocritical Levite along the rocky road to Jericho and succored a needy human being, the vital truth abides. Not until we cease to focus our gaze on the comparatively unimportant, can we discern the great spiritual messages of these early narratives.

The sequel to the great prophetic histories which underlie the Old Testament books, from Genesis through Samuel, is in the books of Kings. These carry the record of Israel's life down to the Babylonian exile. The opening chapters of First Kings contain the conclusion of the Judean prophetic David stories. Fortunately the rest of the biblical history to the exile was largely compiled from much earlier sources. As in most of the historical writings, the later editors, also, quoted verbatim from these earlier records and histories, so that in many cases we have the testimony of almost contemporary witnesses. The titles of certain of these earlier books are given: The Book of the Acts of Solomon, The Chronicles of the Kings of Israel, and The Chronicles of the Kings of Judah.

A careful study of the books of Kings suggests many other ancient sources. For the reign of Solomon, state annals, temple records, and popular Solomon traditions appear to have been utilized. The graphic account of the division of the Hebrew empire was probably drawn from an early Jeroboam history. In the latter part of First Kings appear citations from an early Ahab history and a group of Ephraimite Elijah stories. The political data throughout First and Second Kings were probably drawn from the annals of the northern and southern kingdoms. Furthermore, in II Kings ii.-viii. appear long quotations from two cycles of Elisha stories, centring, respectively, about the ancient northern sanctuary of Gilgal, near Shiloh, and about Samaria. The rest of the book includes citations from sources which may be designated as a prophetic Jehu history, temple records, a Hezekiah history, and a group of Isaiah stories.

These valuable quotations the late prophetic editor of Kings has arranged in chronological order and fitted into a framework which gives the length of each reign and the date of accession of the different kings, according to the chronology of the other Hebrew kingdom. To this data he adds a personal judgment upon the policy of each ruler, thereby revealing his prophetic spirit. History is to him, as to every true prophet, a supreme illustration of fundamental spiritual principles. Clearly the influence that led him to compile and edit his great work was his recognition of the fact that the record of Israel's national experience as a whole was of deep religious import. The same motive undoubtedly guided him in the selection of material from his great variety of sources. Only that which was essential was presented. Thus he, or a later editor of his book, traced Israel's remarkable history down to the middle of the Babylonian exile (560 B.C.), and completed that wonderful chain of prophetic narratives which record and interpret the first great chapter of divine revelation through the chosen race.

VII

THE HISTORY OF THE PROPHETIC SERMONS, EPISTLES, AND APOCALYPSES

To understand and rightly interpret the prophetic writings of the Old Testament it is necessary to cast aside a false impression as to the character of the prophets which is widely prevalent. They were not foretellers, but forth-tellers. Instead of being vague dreamers, in imagination living far in the distant future, they were most emphatically men of their own times, enlightened and devoted patriots, social and ethical reformers, and spiritual teachers. Their characteristic note of conviction and authority was due to the fact that, on the one hand, they knew personally and distinctly the evils and needs of their nation, and that, on the other hand, their minds and hearts, ever open to receive the truth, were in vital touch with the Infinite. Thus, just as Aaron became Moses' prophet to the people, publicly proclaiming what the great leader imparted to him in private (Ex. vii. 1, 2), so the Hebrew prophets became Jehovah's heralds and ambassadors, announcing by word and life and act the divine will.

While the historians were perfecting their histories certain prophets also were beginning to commit their sermons to writing. The oldest recorded address in the Old Testament is probably that of Amos at Bethel. His banishment from the northern kingdom under strict injunction not to prophesy there (Am. vii. 10-17) may well explain why he resorted to writing to give currency to his prophetic message, though, like Paul in later days, he undoubtedly regarded writing as an inferior substitute for the spoken word. Jeremiah appears to have preached twenty years before he dictated a line to his scribe Baruch, and then it was because he could not personally speak in the temple (xxxvi. 1-5). Sometimes complete sermons of the prophets are preserved, but more often we seem to have only extracts and epitomes. In some of the prophetic books, like that of Jeremiah, there are also popular reports of a prophetic address, and narrative sections, telling of the prophet's experience.

Evidences of editing are very apparent in the earlier prophecies. Sudden interruptions, and verses or clauses, in which appear ideas and literary style very different from that of the immediate context, indicate that many of the prophecies have been supplemented by later notes, some explanatory and some hortatory. Other longer passages are intended to adjust the earlier teaching to later conditions and beliefs and so to adapt them to universal human needs that they are not limited to the hour and occasion of their first delivery. Some of these passages come from the hands of disciples of the prophets and often contain valuable additional data; others are from later prophetic editors and scribes. A detailed comparison, for example, of the Hebrew and Greek versions of Jeremiah quickly discloses wide variations of words, verses, and even long passages, added in one or the other text by later hands. All these additions testify to the deep interest felt by later generations in the earlier writings, even before they were assigned a final place in the canon. It is one of the important tasks of biblical scholars to distinguish the original from the additions and thus determine what were the teachings of each prophet and what are the contributions of later generations.

Many of the later additions possess a value and authority entirely independent of that possessed by the prophet with whose writings they have been joined by their original authors or later editors. Thus the sublime chapters appended to the original sermons of Isaiah contain some of the noblest teachings in the Old Testament. The different themes and literary style; the frequent references to the Babylonians, not as distant allies, as in the days of Isaiah the son of Amoz, but as the hated oppressors of the Jews; the evidence that the prophet's readers are not exiles far from Judah; the many allusions to the conquests of Cyrus, — all these leave little doubt that chapters xl.-lv. were written in the latter part of the Babylonian or the first of the Persian period. Interpreted in the light of this background, their thought and teachings become clear and luminous. Similarly, the varied evidence within the chapters themselves seems to indicate that Isaiah lvi.-lxvi. contain sermons directed to the struggling Jewish community in Palestine during the days following the rebuilding of the temple in 520 B.C.

The prophetic sermons, epistles, and apocalypses fall naturally into five great groups. The books prophets of the Assyrian period were Amos and

Hosea, who between 750 and 734 B.C. preached to Northern Israel; also Isaiah and Micah, whose work lies between 740 and 680 B.C. Nahum's little prophecy, although much later, echoes the death-knell of the great Assyrian kingdom, which for two or three centuries dominated southwestern Asia. The prophets of Judah's decline were Zephaniah (about 628 B.C.), Jeremiah (628-690), and Habakkuk (609-605). To the same period belong Ezekiel's earlier sermons, delivered between 592 and 586, just before the final destruction of Jerusalem. The prophets of the Babylonian exile were Obadiah, whose original oracle belongs to its opening years; Ezekiel (xxv.-xlviii.), who continued to preach until 572 B.C., and the great prophet whose deathless messages ring through Isaiah xl.-lv. The prophets of the Persian period were Haggai and Zechariah, whose inspiring sermons kept alive the flagging zeal of those who rebuilt the second temple; the authors of Isaiah lvi.-lxvi.; the author of the little book of Malachi; and Joel. To this list we may perhaps add the prophet who has given us that noble protest, found in the much misunderstood book of Jonah, against the narrow and intolerant attitude of later Judaism toward foreigners.

With the exception of Ezekiel, Haggai, Zechariah, and Joel, all the prophecies which come from the centuries following the fall of Jerusalem in 586 B.C. are anonymous. The worship of the authority of the past had begun, and there is evidence that the belief was gaining currency that the days of the prophets were past. Hence the natural tendency to resort to anonymous authorship or else to append a later message to an earlier prophecy. Chapters ix.-xiv. of the book of Zechariah illustrate this custom, — chapters which apparently come from the last Old Testament period, the Greek or Maccabean. The habit of presenting prophetic truth in the highly figurative, symbolic form, of the apocalypse also became prominent in later Judaism. This has already been noted in the study of the growth of the New Testament, and is illustrated by the book of Revelation. It was especially adapted to periods of religious persecution, for it enabled the prophet to convey his message of encouragement and consolation in language impressive and clear to his people, yet unintelligible to their foreign masters.

To the mind of one who has carefully studied the book of Daniel in the light of the great crisis that came to the Jews as a result of the relentless persecutions of Antiochus Epiphanes, between the years 169 and 165 B.C., there remains little doubt that it is in this period the wonderful apocalypse finds its true setting and interpretation. The familiar examples of the heroic fidelity of Daniel and his friends to the demands of their religion and ritual were supremely well adapted to arouse a similar resistance toward the demands of a tyrant who was attempting to stamp out the Jewish, religion and transform the chosen people into a race of apostates. The visions found in the book trace rapidly, in succession, the history of the Babylonian, Median, Persian, and, last of all, the Greek kingdoms. The culmination is a minute description of the character and reign, of the tyrant Antiochus Epiphanes (xi. 21-45). He is clearly the little horn of chapter viii. But suddenly, in the midst of the account of the persecutions, the descriptions become vague and general. Nor is there any reference to the success of the Maccabean uprising; instead, the prediction is made that Jehovah himself will soon come to establish his Messiah's kingdom.

The inference is, therefore, that the prophecy was written a short time before the rededication of the temple in 165 B.C. This conclusion is confirmed by many other indications. For example the language, in part Aramaic, is that of the Greek period. The mistakes regarding the final overthrow of the Babylonian empire, which was by Cyrus, not Darius, and brought about not by strategy, but as a result of the voluntary submission of the Babylonians, are identical with the errors current in Greek tradition of the same late period. Here, as in the early narratives of Genesis, a true prophet has utilized earlier stories as effective illustrations. He has also given in the common apocalyptic form an interpretation of the preceding four centuries of human history, and showed how through it all God's purpose was being realized, The book concludes with the firm assurance that those who now prove faithful are to be richly rewarded and to have a part in Ms coming Messianic kingdom.

Thus, from the minds of the prophets come the earliest writings of the Old Testament. They consist of exhortations, warnings, messages of encouragement, or else stories intended to illustrate a religious principle or to present, in concrete form, a prophetic ideal. The fundamental motive which produced them all was identical with that which led the disciples and apostles to write the Gospels and Epistles of the New. In the case of the historico-prophetic writings, like Samuel and Kings, the desire to inspire and mould the minds and wills of their readers was combined with the desire to preserve in permanent form a record of the events which, in their national history, revealed most clearly Jehovah's character and purpose. In this respect they correspond perfectly to the Gospels and Acts of the New Testament. It is easy to see, therefore, that kindred aims and ideals actuated these unknown prophetic writers and their later successors, Matthew, Mark, and Luke. Their literary products differ only because their subject-matter is different. The one group records Jehovah's revelation of himself through the life of the Messianic nation, the other through the life of the perfect Messiah.

It is interesting to note, in conclusion, that from the point of view of the Old, all the literature of the New may be designated as prophetic. The three distinct groups of writings found in the New, namely, the Gospels and Acts, the Epistles, and the Apocalypse, correspond exactly to the three types of prophetic literature found in the Old: the historico-prophetical writings, direct written prophecies, and apocalypses. If the final canon of the Old Testament had been completed before the days of Josiah, there is every reason to believe that it also would have contained little beside prophetic writings. In divine providence it was not closed until seven centuries later, so that, as it has come to us, it is a comprehensive library, representing every stage and every side of Israel's development. It is, however, in perfect keeping with the spirit of the Master that the New Testament should contain significant facts and broad principles rather than detailed laws or even the songs of worship. He whose ideals, teachings, and methods were in closest harmony with those of the Hebrew prophets, naturally begat, through his immediate followers, a group of distinctively prophetic writings.

VIII

THE DEVELOPMENT OF THE EARLIER OLD TESTAMENT LAWS

If the canon of the New Testament had remained open as long as did that of the Old, there is little doubt that it also would have contained many laws, legal precedents, and ecclesiastical histories. From the writings of the Church Fathers and the records of the Catholic Church it is possible to conjecture what these in general would have been. The early history of Christianity illustrates the universal fact that the broad principles are first enunciated by a great prophetic leader or leaders, and that in succeeding centuries these new principles are gradually embodied in detailed laws and ceremonials. Also the principles must be accepted, partially at least, by the majority of the people before the enactments based upon them can be enforced. This important fact, stated in Old Testament terms, is that the prophet must and always does precede the lawgiver.

Torah, the common Hebrew word for law, comes from a Hebrew word meaning to point out or direct. It is probably also connected with the older root signifying, to cast the sacred lot. The torah, therefore, was originally the decision, rendered in connection with specific questions of dispute, and referred to Jehovah by means of the sacred lot. Thus the early priests were also judges because they were the custodians of the divine oracle.

Origin of this Hebrew belief in the divine origin of law

Here we are able to trace, in its earliest Hebrew form, the universal belief in the divine origin of the law. In the primitive laws of Exodus xxi.-xxiii., in connection with a case of disputed responsibility for injury to property, the command is given: the cause of both parties shall come before God; he whom God shall condemn shall pay double to his neighbor (xxii. 8, 9). In ancient times all cases of dispute were thus laid before God and decided by the lot or by God's representatives, usually the priests. When, in time, customs and oral laws grew up on the basis of these decisions, a similar divine origin and authority were naturally attributed to them. Individually and collectively they were designated by the same suggestive term, torah. When they were ultimately committed to writing, the legal literature bore this title. In the Hebrew text it still remains as the designation of the first group of Old Testament books which contain the bulk of Israel's laws.

A belief in the divine origin of law was held by most ancient peoples. In connection with the tablet which records the laws of Hammurabi, we have a picture of Shamash the sun-god giving the laws to the king. In the epilogue to these laws he states that by the command of Shamash, the judge supreme of heaven and earth, he has set them up that judgment may shine in the land. The statements in the Old Testament that Jehovah talked face to face with Moses or wrote the ten words with his finger on tablets of stone reflect the primitive belief which pictured God as a man with hands and voice and physical body; still they are the early concrete statement of a vital, eternal truth. Not on perishable stone, but in the minds of the ancient judges, and in the developing ethical consciousness of the Israelitish race, he inscribed the principles of which the laws are the practical expression. If he had not revealed them, there would have been no progress in the knowledge of justice and mercy. The thesis of the Old Testament, and of Hammurabi also, is fundamentally true. The vivid forms in which both expressed that thesis were admirably fitted to impress it upon the mind of early man.

The early Israelitish theory of the origin, of law provided fully for expansion and development to meet the new and changed conditions of later periods. Whenever a new question presented itself, it could be referred to Jehovah's representatives, the priests and prophets; and their torah, or response, would forthwith become the basis for the new law. Malachi ii. 6,7 clearly defines this significant element in the growth, of Israel's legal codes: the torah of truth was in the mouth of the priest… and the people should seek the torah at his mouth. Similarly Haggai commands the people to ask a torah from the priests in regard to a certain question of ceremonial cleanliness (ii, 11). Until a very late period in Israelitish history, the belief was universal that Jehovah was ever giving new decisions and laws through his priests and prophets, and therefore that the law itself was constantly being expanded and developed. This belief is in perfect accord with all historical analogies and with the testimony of the Old Testament histories and laws themselves. Not until the days of the latest editors did the tendency to project the Old Testament laws back to the beginning of Israel's history gain the ascendency and leave its impression upon the Pentateuch. Even then there was no thought of attributing the literary authorship of all of these laws to Moses. This was the work of still later Jewish tradition.

The earliest Old Testament narratives indicate clearly the real historical basis of the familiar later tradition, and vindicate and help us in the effort to define the title,Law of Moses. The early Ephraimite narratives describe Moses as a prophet rather than as a mere lawgiver. In Exodus xviii. they give us a vivid picture of his activity as judge. To him the people came in crowds, with their cases, to inquire of God (15). In 16, to his father-in-law Jethro, he states: whenever they have a matter of dispute they come to me, that I may decide which of the two is right, and make known the statutes of God and his decisions (tôrôth). Jethro then advises him to appoint reliable men, gifted with a high sense of justice, to decide minor cases, while he reserves for himself the difficult questions involving new principles. The origin and theory of Israel's early laws are vividly presented in Jethro's words to Moses in verses 19, 20: You be the people's advocate with God, and bring the cases to God, and you make known to them the statutes and the decisions, and show them the way wherein they must walk, and the work that they must do.

It appears from these and other passages that Moses' traditional title as the father of Israelitish legislation is well established. As a prophet, he proclaimed certain fundamental principles that became the basis of all later codes. As a judge, he rendered decisions that soon grew into customary laws. As a leader and organizer, he laid the foundations of the later political and institutional growth of the nation. Furthermore, it is probable that he taught the people certain simple commands which became the nucleus of all later legislation. Naturally and properly, as oral laws subsequently grew up and were finally committed to writing, they were attributed to him. Later, when these laws were collected and codified, they were still designated as Mosaic, even, though the authors of these codes added many contemporary enactments to the earlier laws. Thus the traditions, as well as the theory, of Israelitish law fortunately raised no barrier against its normal growth. It was not until the late Jewish period, when the tradition became rigid and unnatural, that the rabbis, in order to establish the authority of contemporary laws, were forced to resort to the grotesque legal fictions which appear in the Talmud.

The earliest Hebrew laws, like the traditions, were apparently long transmitted in oral form. The simple life of the desert and early Canaan required no written records. Custom and memory preserved all the laws that were needed. Also, as we have seen, before the Hebrews came into contact with the Canaanites and Phoenicians, they do not seem to have developed the literary art. Instead, they cast their important commands and laws into the form of pentads and decalogues. The practical aim seems to have been to aid the memory by associating a brief law with each finger of the two hands. The system was both simple and effective. It also points clearly to a period of oral rather than written transmission.

The nucleus of all Israelitish law appears to have been a simple decalogue, which gave the terms of the original covenant between Jehovah and his people, and definitely stated the obligations they must discharge if they would retain his favor. The oldest version of this decalogue is now embedded in the early Judean narrative of Exodus xxxiv. There is considerable evidence, however, that it once stood immediately after the Judean account of Jehovah's revelation of himself at Sinai, and was transposed to its present position in order to give place for the later and nobler prophetic decalogue of Exodus xx. 1-17. Its antiquity and importance are also evidenced by the fact that it has received many later introductory, explanatory, and hortatory notes. Exodus xxxiy. 28 preserves the memory that it originally consisted of simply ten words. The slightly variant version of these original ten words Is also found in Exodus xx. 23, xxiii. 12, 15, 16, 18, 29, 30. Furthermore, it probably once occupied a central position in the corresponding Northern Israelltish account of the covenant at Sinai.

With the aid of these two different versions, that of the North and that of the South, it is possible to restore approximately the common original:

I. Thou shalt worship no other God.

II. Thou shalt make no molten gods,

III. Thou shalt observe the feast of unleaven bread.

IV. Every first-born is mine.

V. Six days shalt thou toil, but on the seventh thou shalt rest.

VI. Thou shalt observe the feast of weeks and ingathering at the end of the year,

VII. Thou shalt not offer the blood of my sacrifice with leaven. VIII.

The fat of my feast shall not be left until morning.

IX. The best of the first-fruits of thy land shalt thou bring to the house of Jehovah.

X. Thou shalt not seethe a kid in its mother's milk.

These laws bear on their face the evidence of their primitive date and origin. They define religion not in the terms of life, as does the familiar prophetic decalogue of Exodus xx., but, like the old Babylonian religion, in the terms of the ritual. Loyalty to Jehovah, as the God of the nation, and fidelity to the demands of the cult is their watchword. Their antiquity and the central position they occupy in Old Testament legislation are shown further by the fact that all of them are again quoted in other codes, and most of them four or five times in the Old Testament. Three of them apply to agricultural life; but agriculture is not entirely unknown to the nomadic life of the wilderness. Possibly in their present form certain of these commands have been adapted to conditions in Canaan, but the majority reflect the earliest stages in Hebrew history. In all probability the decalogue in its original form came from Moses, as the earliest traditions assert, although comparative Semitic religion demonstrates that many of the institutions here reflected long antedated the days of the great leader.

Although in part contemporary, the next stage in the development of Israelitish law is represented by the civil, social, and humane decalogues in Exodus xx. 28 to xxiii. 19. The best preserved group is found in xxi.1 to xxii.20, and bears the title Judgments, which recalls Hammurabi's title to his code, The Judgments of Righteousness. Like this great Babylonian code, the Hebrew Judgments deal with civil and social cases, and are usually introduced by the formula, If so and so, followed by the penalty or decision to be rendered. They are evidently intended primarily for the guidance of judges. The parallels with the code of Hammurabi are many, both in theme, form, and penalty, although there is no conclusive evidence that the Hebrew borrowed directly from the older Babylonian. Undoubtedly many of the striking points of resemblance are due simply to common Semitic ideas and institutions and to the recurrence of similar questions. But on the whole, the Hebrew laws place a higher estimate on life and less on property. They reflect also a simpler type of civilization than the Babylonian.

When three or four obviously later additions have been removed, the Judgments are found to consist of five decalogues, each divided into two pentads which deal with different phases of the same general subject. They are as follows:

First Decalogue: The Rights of Slaves.

First Pentad: Males, Ex. xxi. 2,3a, 3b, 4,5-6. Second Pentad: Females, xxi. 7, 8, 9,10, 11.

Second Decalogue: Assaults.

First Pentad: Capital Offences, xxi. 12, 13,14, 15, 16.

Second Pentad: Minor Offences, xxi. 18-19, 20, 21, 26, 27.

Third Decalogue: Laws regarding Domestic Animals.

First Pentad: Injuries by Animals, xxi. 28, 29, 30, 31, 32.

Second Pentad: Injuries to Animals, xxi. 33-34, 35, 36; xxii. 1,4.

Fourth Decalogue: Responsibility for Property.

First Pentad: In General, xxii. 5, 6, 7, 8, 9.

Second Pentad: In Cattle, xxii. 10-11, 13, 14, 15a, 15b.

Fifth Decalogue: Social Purity.

First Pentad: Adultery, Deut. xxii. 13-19, 20-21, 22, 23-24, 25-27.

Second Pentad: Fornication and Apostasy, Ex. xxii. 16, 17, 18, 19, 20.

Many of these laws anticipate the settled agricultural conditions of Palestine. Society, however, is very simple. The decalogue and peatad form also points clearly to an early period, when the laws were transmitted orally. Many of the laws probably came from the days of the wilderness wandering, and therefore go back to the age of Moses, in some cases much earlier, as is shown by close analogies with the code of Hammurabi. Although in their present written form these oral Judgments bear the marks of the Northern Israelitish prophetic writers who have preserved them, the majority, if not all, may with confidence be assigned to the days of David and Solomon.

The remaining verses of Exodus xx. 23 to xxiii. 19, contain, groups of humane and ceremonial laws. In the process of transmission they have been somewhat disarranged, but, with the aid of the fuller duplicate versions in Deuteronomy, four complete decalogues can be restored and part of a fifth. The following analysis will suggest their general character and contents:

HUMANE AND CEREMONIAL LAWS

First Decalogue: Kindness.

First Pentad: Towards Men, Ex. xxii. 21a, 22-23, 25a, 25b, 26-27.

Second Pentad; Towards Animals, Ex, xxiii. 4 Deut. xxii. 1, Deut. xxii. 2, 3; Ex. xxiii. 5

Deut. xxii. 4, Deut. xxii. 6-7.

Second Decalogue: Justice.

First Pentad: Among Equals, Ex. xxiii. 1a, 1b, 2a, 2b, 3.

Second Pentad: On the Part of those in Authority, xxiii, 6, 7a, 7b, 7c, 8.

Third Decalogue: Duties to God.

First Pentad: Worship, Ex. xx. 23a, 23b, 24, 25, 26.

Second Pentad: Loyalty, Ex. xxii. 28, 29a, 29b, 30, 31.

Fourth Decalogue: Sacred Seasons.

First Pentad: Command to Observe them, xxiii. 10-11, 12, l5a, 16a, 16b.

Second Pentad: Method of Observing them, xxiii, 17, 18a, 18b, 19a, 19b.

Here the primitive ceremonial decalogue has been expanded into the third and fourth group given above. Like the Judgments, these decalogues bear testimony to their northern origin, and probably they also have had much the same history, although their relation to the primitive decalogue and the fact that they are prefixed and added to the solid group of Judgments, would seem to indicate that they were somewhat later. These two collections, together with their older prototype, the ancient decalogue, represent the growth of Israel's laws during the four centuries beginning with Moses and extending to about 800 B. C. To distinguish them from later collections they may be designated as the Primitive Codes.

The eighth and seventh centuries before Christ which brought to the Hebrews great crises and revolutionary changes in both their political and religious life, witnessed the epoch-making work of Amos, Hosea, Isaiah, and Micah. This remarkable group of prophets proclaimed so many new principles that a fundamental revision and expansion of Israel's primitive codes became necessary in order to adapt the latter to the new needs of the age. The reactionary reign of Manasseh had also brought out plainly the contrast between the older heathen cults, still cherished by the people, and the exalted ideals of the true prophets. If the prophetic teachings were to become operative in the life of the nation, it was also seen that they must be expressed in concrete legal enactments, which could be universally understood and definitely enforced.

Accordingly, a group of prophets, disciples of the older masters, and inspired by the spirit of reform, devoted themselves to this all-important task. The results of their work are represented by the prophetic law-book of Deuteronomy. Through its pages glow the new ethical teachings of the prophets of the Assyrian period. The elements of Hosea's doctrine, love to

God and love to men and kindness to the needy and oppressed, in their new setting and application, make it one of the evangels of the Old Testament. Its lofty standards of justice and social responsibility reflect the impassioned addresses of Amos and Hosea. Since the new laws, as a whole, represented the practical application of the messages of the prophets to life, they were justly and appropriately placed in the mouth of Moses, the real and traditional head of the nation and of the prophetic order.

A comparison of this prophetic law-book with the older primitive laws shows that the latter were made the basis of the new codes, since most of them, in revised form, are also found in Deuteronomy. The prophetic lawmakers, however, in the same spirit that actuated Jesus in his attitude toward the ancient law, freely modified, supplemented, and in some cases substituted for the primitive enactments, laws that more perfectly embodied the later revelation.

The nature of the reforms instituted by Josiah, according to II Kings xxii., clearly prove that the laws which inspired them were those of Deuteronomy, and that this was the law-book discovered in the temple by Hilkiah the priest and publicly read and promulgated by the king in 621 B.C. Originally it was probably prepared by the prophetic reformers as a basis for their work; but it incorporates not only most of the primitive codes, but also many other ancient laws and groups of laws, some doubtless coming from the earliest periods of Israel's history. It also appears to have been further supplemented after the reformation of Josiah. In general it represents the second great stage in Old Testament law, as it rapidly developed between 800 and 600 B.C. under the inspiring preaching of the remarkable prophets of the Assyrian period.

These laws represent, in many ways, the high-water mark of Old Testament legislation. Every effort is made to eliminate that which experience had proved to be imperfect in the older laws and customs. The chief aim is to protect the rights of the wronged and dependent. The appeal throughout is not to the fear of punishment — in a large number of laws no penalty is suggested — but to the individual conscience. Not merely formal worship is demanded, but a love to God so personal that it dominates the individual heart and soul and finds expression through energies completely devoted to his service. These laws required strict justice, but more than that, mercy and practical charity toward the weak and needy and afflicted. Even the toiling ox and the helpless mother-bird and her young are not beyond the kin of these wonderful laws. Under their benign influence the divine principles of the prophets began to mould directly the character and life of the Israelitish race. The man who lives in accord with their spirit and injunctions to-day finds himself on the straight and narrow way, hallowed by the feet of the Master.

IX

INFLUENCES THAT GAVE RISE TO THE PRIESTLY LAWS AND HISTORIES

The Babylonian exile gave a great opportunity and incentive to the further development of written law. While the temple stood, the ceremonial rites and customs received constant illustration, and were transmitted directly from father to son in the priestly families. Hence, there was little need of writing them down. But when most of the priests were carried captive to Babylonia, as in 597 B.C., and ten years later the temple was laid in ruins and all sacrifice and ceremonial worship suddenly ceased, written records at once became indispensable, if the customs and rules of Israel's ritual were to be preserved. The integrity and future of the scattered Israelitish race also largely depended upon keeping alive their distinctive traditions. Torn from their altars, the exiled priests not only had a strong incentive, but likewise the leisure, to write. The ritualistic zeal of their Babylonian masters doubtless further inspired them. The result was, that during the Babylonian exile and the following century most of the ceremonial laws in the Old Testament appear to have been first committed to writing.

Even Ezekiel, the prophet of the early exile, yielded to the influence of his early priestly training and the needs of the situation. In 572 he issued the unique code found in chapters xl.-xlviii. of his prophecy. It provides for the rebuilding of the temple, and defines the duties of its different officials and the form of ritual that is to be observed. The whole is intended primarily to emphasize, through the arrangement of the sanctuary and the forms of the ceremonial, the transcendent holiness of Jehovah. Ezekiel also proclaims, through this elaborate program for the restored community, the certainty that the exiles would be allowed to return and rebuild the temple. He evidently reproduces many of the proportions and regulations of the first temple, but, with the same freedom that characterizes the authors of the Deuteronomic codes, he unhesitatingly sets aside earlier usages where something better has been revealed.

Ezekiel's code was never fully adopted by the later Jews, for much of it was symbolic rather than practical; but it powerfully influenced subsequent lawmakers, and was indicative of the dominant tendency of the day. Even before he issued his code, some like-minded priest had collected and arranged an important group of laws, which appear to have been familiar to Ezekiel himself. They are found in Leviticus xvii.-xxvi., and have felicitously been designated as the Holiness Code, because they constantly emphasize the holiness of Jehovah and the necessity of the people's being holy in thought and act. In chapters xvii.-xix. most of the original laws are still arranged in the decalogue and pentad form. This strong evidence that they had been transmitted by word of mouth from a much earlier period is supported by their contents. They resemble and supplement the primitive laws of Exodus xx. 23 to xxiii. 19. Many of them probably came from the early periods of Israelitish history. Most of the laws, like those of the prophetic codes in Deuteronomy, are ethical and humane rather than ceremonial. The code, as a whole, is a remarkable combination of prophetic and priestly teaching. It marks the transition from the age of the prophets, represented by Deuteronomy, to that of the priests and ritual, represented by the priestly codes proper. Like every important early collection of laws, It also has been much supplemented by later editors; the original Holiness Code, however, may be given a date soon after the first captivity in 597 B.C.

The influences represented by Ezekiel and the Holiness Code have given us the remaining laws of the Old Testament. These are found in Leviticus i.-xvi., xxviii., and, excepting Exodus xx.-xxiii., xxxiv., in the legal sections of Exodus and Numbers. They deal almost entirely with such ceremonial subjects, as the forms and rules of sacrifice, the observation of the annual religious festivals, and the rights and duties of priests. Many of them incorporated laws and customs as old or older than the days of Moses. An early and important group, technically known as the Priestly teaching (Lev. i.-iii., v.-vii., xi.-xv.; Num. v., vi., xv., xix. 14-22), is repeatedly designated asthe torah of the burnt-offering (Lev. vi. 9), or the torah of the meal-offering (vi, 14), or the torah of the unclean and clean beast or bird (xi. 46, 47). It is evidently based upon the toroth, or decisions, rendered by the priests concerning the various ceremonial questions thus treated. The recurring phrase, according to the ordinance, probably refers to the fixed usage observed in connection with the first temple.

The atmosphere and point of view of these priestly laws as a whole are the exilic and post-exilic periods. The ritual has become much more elaborate, the position of the priests much more prominent, and their income far greater than before the exile. The distinction between priest and Levite, which was not recognized before the exile, is clearly defined. The annual feasts have increased, and their old joyous character has largely disappeared under the dark shadow of the exile. Sin-offerings, guilt-offerings, trespass-offerings, and the day of atonement (practically unknown before the fall of Jerusalem in 586 B.C.) reflect the spirit of the later Judaism which sought to win Jehovah's favor by its many sacrifices. Within these priestly codes there is also evidence of development. The older collections, such as the priestly teachings, were probably made early in the Babylonian exile. Others represent the gradual expansion and supplementing of these older groups, the process apparently continuing until the days of Nehemiah and Ezra. The whole, therefore, is the fruit of the remarkable priestly literary activity between 600 and 400 B.C., and possibly extending even later.

The Jewish community which Nehemiah found in Palestine was still living under the Deuteronomic law, and apparently knew nothing of the very different demands of the priestly codes. His reform measures recorded in Nehemiah v. and xiii., as well as his effective work in repairing the walls, prepared the way for the sweeping innovations which followed the public acceptance of the new law-book, brought according to tradition by Ezra. Five out of the eight regulations specified by the oath then taken by the leaders of the nation (Neh. x. 30-39) are found only in the priestly codes; one of them, indeed, is not presented elsewhere in the Old Testament. Henceforth the life of the Jewish race is moulded by these later codes. It is, therefore, safe to conclude that they constituted the essence of the new law-book solemnly adopted by the Jewish community as its guide somewhere about 400 B.C.

Inasmuch as the interest of the priests centred in ceremonial institutions and the history of the law rather than about individuals and politics, it was natural that they also should write their own history of the race. Their general purpose was to give an introduction and setting to their laws. As might be anticipated, this priestly history incorporates the traditions of the late priestly school, and therefore those current long centuries after the events recorded transpired. As in the case of the prophetic narratives, the aim is not primarily historical, but doctrinal. The peculiar vocabulary, language, and theological conceptions are those which distinguish the post-exilic priestly editors of the latest Old Testament laws.

Their history begins with the majestic account of creation in Genesis i. 1 to ii. 4a. God does not form man from the dust, as in the primitive prophetic account, but by a simple word of command; and by progressive acts of creation he realizes his perfect plan, which culminates in the creation of mankind. The literary style is that of a legalist: formal, precise, repetitious, and generic. The ultimate aim of the narrative is to trace the origin of the institution of the Sabbath back to the creation. The genealogical history of Genesis v. connects this account of creation with the priestly version of the flood story which leads up to the covenant with Noah. The priestly genealogical histories of Genesis x. and xi. 10-27 trace the ancestry of the Hebrews through Abraham. Regarding this patriarch these later historians present only a brief sketch; in Genesis xvii., however, they expand their narrative to give in detail the origin of the rite of circumcision, which they associate with him. Jacob is to them chiefly of interest as the father of the ten tribes.

The history of the experiences of the Hebrews in Egypt is briefly outlined as the prelude to the traditional institution of the feast of the passover. Sinai, however, is the great goal of the priestly narratives, for about it they group all their laws. It is their concrete method of proclaiming the antiquity and divine origin of Israelitish legislation. The period of the wilderness wandering is also made the background of many important legal precedents. The priestly history concludes with an account of the conquest of Canaan and the allotment of the territory to the different tribes.

In these late priestly narratives the historical perspective is sometimes considerably shortened and sometimes lengthened. Moreover, their representation often differs widely from that of the parallel but much earlier prophetic histories. The original traditions have also assumed larger proportions, and the supernatural element is much more prominent. This is evidently the result of long transmission, in an age that had largely lost the historic sense, and among the priestly exiles, who were far removed from the real life of Palestine.

The wide variations between the older prophetic and late priestly accounts of the same events might be illustrated by scores of examples. The following parallel account of the exodus will suffice:

Ex. xiv. l9b. Then the pillar of cloud changed its position from before them and stood behind them. (20b) And the cloud lighted up the night; yet throughout the entire night the one army did not come near the other. (21b) And Jehovah caused the sea to go back by a strong east wind all the night, and made the bed of the sea dry. (24b) And it came to pass in the watch before the dawn that Jehovah looked forth through the pillar of fire and of cloud upon the host of the Egyptians, (25) and he bound their horsemen.

(21a, c) Then Moses stretched out his hand over the sea, and the waters were divided, (22) so that the Israelites went into the midst of the sea on the dry ground; and the waters were a wall to them on their right hand and on their left. (23b) And the Egyptians went in after them into the midst of the sea, all Pharaoh's horses, his chariots, and his horsemen. (26) Then Jehovah said to Moses, Stretch out thy hand over the sea, that the waters may come again upon the Egyptians, upon their chariots and their chariot wheels, so that they proceeded with difficulty. Then the Egyptians said, Let us flee from before Israel; for Jehovah fighteth for them against the Egyptians. (27b) But the sea returned to its ordinary level toward morning, while the Egyptians were flying before it. And Jehovah shook off the Egyptians into the midst of the sea, (28b) so that not one of them remained. (30) Thus Jehovah saved Israel that day out of the power of the Egyptians; and Israel saw the Egyptians dead upon the sea-shore.

(27a) So Moses stretched forth his hand over the sea, (28a) and the waters returned and covered the chariots, and the horsemen, even all the host of Pharaoh that went in after them into the sea. (29) But the Israelites walked upon dry land in the midst of the sea, the waters being a wall to them on their right hand, and on their left. "Student's Old Testament," Vol. I., 175, 176.

No one can doubt for a moment that the older, simpler, and more natural version is, from the historical point of view, the more accurate. The normal man to-day has outgrown the craving for the grotesquely supernatural. The omnipotent, omniscient, loving Creator, who reveals himself through the growing flower, commands our admiration as fully as a God who speaks through the unusual and extraordinary. Everything is possible with God, and the man is blind indeed who would deny the Infinite Being, who is all and in all, the ability to pass beyond the bounds of that which we, with our extremely limited vision, have designated as natural. The real question is, How did God see fit to accomplish his ends? Our judicial and historical sense unhesitatingly inclines to the older and simpler narratives as containing the true answer. In distinguishing these different strands of narrative, it must be acknowledged that modern biblical scholarship has performed a service invaluable alike to the student of literature, of history, and of revelation.

In passing, it is instructive to note that, almost without exception, Ingersoll's once famous examples of the mistakes of Moses were drawn from the priestly narratives. It is safe to predict that had that learned jurist been introduced, when a boy, to the Old Testament, as revealed in modern light, he would have enjoyed a very different popular fame. In the divine economy, however, even the sledge-hammer of ridicule may play an important rôle in shattering false claims and the untenable theories which obscure the real truth. It is wholesome to apply the principle of relative values to the Bible, since one cannot fully appreciate the best without recognizing that which is inferior. These priestly narratives come from a school which, in its reverence for the form and the letter, had began to lose sight of the vital and spiritual. Its still later product is that ritualistic

Judaism which stands in such unfavorable contrast to the perfected spiritual revelation which came through Jesus. At the same time, the recognition of the defects of the late priestly school should not deter us from appreciating the rich religious teaching of a narrative like the first chapter of Genesis, nor from accepting its great message, namely, that through all natural phenomena and history God is revealing and perfecting his gracious purpose.

The long ecclesiastical history found in I and II Chronicles and the original sequel of these books, Ezra and Nehemiah, were written from the same general point of view as the late priestly narratives, but in a much later period. The same peculiar literary style and conceptions, which recur throughout these four books, show clearly that they are from one author and age. Since they trace the history to the beginning of the Greek period and speak of the kings and events of the Persian period as if they belonged to the distant past, it is evident that the anonymous author, who is usually designated as the Chronicler, lived after the conquests of Alexander. The internal evidence all points to the middle of the third century before Christ as the date of their composition.

From the author's evident interest in the ritual of the temple, and especially its song service, it would appear that he belonged to one of the guilds of temple singers that became prominent in the post-exilic period. His history centres about the sanctuary and its services. Since Judah, not Israel, is the land of the temple, Northern Israel is almost completely ignored. Like the late priestly historians, his chief aim is to trace the origin of the ceremonial institutions back to the beginnings of Hebrew history. Thus he represents the song service and the guilds of singers as having been established in the days of David. Living as he did under the glamour of the great Persian and Greek empires, he, in common with his contemporaries, idealized the past glories of his race. As we compare his versions of early events with the older parallel accounts of Samuel and Kings, we find that iron has become gold, and hundreds have become thousands, and defeats are transformed into victories. No mention is made of the crimes of such kings as David and

Solomon, since they are venerated profoundly as the founders of the temple.

The basis of I and II Chronicles is the prophetic history of Samuel and Kings; from these the author quotes verbatim chapter after chapter, according as their contents are adapted to his purpose. This groundwork he supplements by introducing the priestly traditions current in his own day. Possibly he quotes also from certain somewhat earlier written collections of traditions, for to those, following the example of the author of Kings, he frequently refers his readers for further information. In some cases these later traditions may have preserved authentic, supplemental data; but when the representation of Chronicles differs, as it frequently does, from that of Samuel and Kings, the older and more sober prophetic history is undoubtedly to be followed.

In Ezra and Nehemiah the author has preserved some exceedingly valuable historical material, for he has quoted, fortunately, long sections from two or three older sources. Oae is the document in Ezra iv. 7 to vi. 14, the original Aramaic of which is retained. This appears to have been a temple record, dating from the middle or latter part of the Persian period, and tells of the interruption of the temple building in the days of Darius and the finding of the original decree of Cyrus sanctioning the restoration of the shrine of Jerusalem. Still more important is the wonderful memoir of Nehemiah quoted in Nehemiah i., ii., iv. to vii. 5, xii. 31, 32, 37-40, and xiii. 4-31. Here we are able to study the events of an exceedingly important period through the eyes of the man who, by his able and self-sacrificing efforts, did more than any one else to develop and shape later Judaism. Less important, yet suggestive, citations are taken from the priestly traditions regarding the work of Ezra. The final editor has apparently rearranged this material in order to give to the work of Ezra the scribe such precedence over that of Nehemiah the layman, as, from his later Levitical point of view, he deemed proper. Restoring what seems to have been the original order (i.e., Ezra vii. viii., Neh. vii. 70 to viii. 18; Ezra ix., x.; Neh. ix., x.) and studying it as the sequel of Nehemiah's essential pioneer work, the obscurities of this period begin to disappear and its significant facts to stand out in clear relief.

Thus we find that, quoting largely as he does, from much older sources, the author of this great ecclesiastical history of Judah and the temple has given us, in Ezra and Nehemiah, some exceedingly important historical data. His writings also clearly reveal the ideas and institutions of his own day; but otherwise it is not as history that his work is of permanent value. Rather it is because, in common with all the great teachers who speak to us through the Old Testament, he believed firmly in the moral order of the universe, and that back of all events and all history is an infinitely powerful yet just and merciful God who is constantly revealing himself to mankind. While these later priestly writers were not in such close touch with fact and life as were the prophets, and while they were subject to the defects of all extreme ritualists and theologians, they were faithful heralds of truth to their own and later generations. Behind their symbolism and traditions lie certain great universal principles which amply reward an earnest quest.

X

THE HEBREW SAGES AND THEIR PROVERBS

In the days of Jeremiah and Ezekiel (Jer. xviii. 18; Ezek. vii. 26) three distinct classes of religious teachers were recognized by the people: the prophets, the priests, and the wise men or sages. From their lips and pens have come practically all the writings of the Old Testament. Of these three classes the wise men or sages are far less prominent or well known. They wrote no history of Israel, they preached no public sermons, nor do they appear to have been connected with any sanctuaries. Quietly, as private teachers, they appealed to the nation through the consciences and wills of individuals. Proverbs viii. 1-5 reveals their methods:

Doth not wisdom cry,

And understanding put forth her voice?

On the top of high places by the way,

Where the paths meet, she standeth;

Beside the gates, at the entry of the city,

At the coining in at the doors, she crieth aloud:

Unto you, O men, I call;

And my voice is to the sons of men.

O ye simple, understand prudence;

And ye fools, be of an understanding heart.

At the open spaces beside the city gates, where legal cases were tried, at the intersections of the streets, wherever men congregated, the sages of ancient Israel could be found, ready and eager to instruct or advise the inexperienced and foolish.

The wise man or sage is a characteristic Oriental figure. First Kings iv. 30 speaks of the far-famed wisdom of the nomadic tribes of northern Arabia and of the wisdom of Egypt. The sage appears to have been the product of the early nomadic Semitic life, in which books were unknown and the practical wisdom gained by experience was treasured in the minds of certain men who were called the wise or sages. In our more complex western life such functions have been distributed among the members of the legal, medical, and clerical professions, but even now, in smaller towns, may be found an Uncle Toby who is the counterpart of the ancient Hebrew sage. To men of this type young and old resort with their private problems, and rarely return without receiving real help and light. In the East, sages are still to be found, usually gray-bearded elders, honored and influential in the tribe or town.

Of the three classes of Israel's teachers the sages stood in closest touch with the people. They were naturally the father-confessors of the community. Observation was their guide, enlightened common sense their interpreter, and experience their teacher. The great book of human life, which is one of the most important chapters of divine revelation, was thrown open wide before them. The truths that they read there, as their eyes were divinely opened to see it, are recorded in the wisdom books of the Old Testament, — Proverbs, Job, The Song of Songs, and Ecclesiastes.

It is significant that neither Israel nor the nation is mentioned in all the wisdom literature, and that man is spoken of thirty-three times in the book of Proverbs alone. Man was the object of their study and teaching; the nation, only as it was made up of individuals. In this respect the sages stand in contrast with the prophets, whose message usually is to the nation. They also have little to say about the ritual or the forms of religion. To them the fear and knowledge of God is the beginning of wisdom, and its end a normal relation to God, to one's fellowmen, and to life. Their message is directed equally to all mankind. The subjects that command, their attention are of universal interest: the nature and tendencies of man, and his relations and duties to God, to society, to the family, and to himself. Everything that concerns man, whether it be the tilling of the soil, the choice of a wife, the conduct of a lawsuit, or the proper deportment in the presence of a ruler, commands their earnest consideration.

The Hebrew sages, however, were not mere students of human nature or philosophers. Knowledge to them was not an end in itself, but only a means. Their contribution to Israel's life was counsel (Jer. xviii. 18). Their aim was, by the aid of their tried maxims, to so advise the inexperienced, the foolish, indeed, all who needed advice, that they might live the fullest and best lives and successfully attain all worthy ends. While their teaching was distinctively ethical and religious, it was also very practical and utilitarian. As pastors and advisers of the people, they drew their principles and ideals from Israel's prophets, and applied them to the practical, every-day problems of life. It is obvious that without their patient, devoted instruction the preparation of the chosen people for their mission would have been imperfect, and that without a record of their teachings the Old Testament would have been incomplete.

The proverb was the most characteristic literary form in which the sages treasured and imparted their teachings. Poetical in structure, terse, often figurative or epigrammatic, the proverb was well calculated to arouse individual thought and make a deep impression on the mind. Transmitted from mouth to mouth for many generations, like the popular tradition or law, it lost by attrition all its unnecessary elements, so that, 'like an arrow,' it shot straight to the mark. Based on common human experience, it found a ready response in the heart of man. In this way crystallized experience was transmitted, gathering effectiveness and volume in each succeeding generation. Job viii. 8-10 speaks of this accumulated wisdom handed down from the former age, that which the fathers have searched out. They shall teach man and inform him, and utter words out of their heart. Job xv. 18 also refers to that which wise men have told from their fathers and have not hid it. A proverb thus orally transmitted not only gains in beauty of form but also in authority, for it is constantly being tested in the laboratory of real life and receives the silent attestation of thousands of men and of many different generations.

When the sages desired to treat a many-sided subject, as, for example, intemperance, they still used proverbs, but combined them into brief gnomic essays (e. g., xxiii. 29-85, xxvi. 1-17). Sometimes, to fix the attention of their hearers, they combined two proverbs, so as to produce a paradox, as in Proverbs xxvi. 4, 5:

Answer not a fool according to his folly,

Lest them also be like unto him.

Answer a fool according to his folly,

Lest he be wise in his own conceit.

Later they developed the simple gnomic essay into a philosophical drama, of which Job is the classic example, or into a homily, like Ecclesiastes.

Side by side with the proverb, the sages appear from the earliest times to have used the fable also; this is illustrated by the fable of Jotham in Judges ix. 6-21. Of the riddle a famous examples is that of Samson in Judges xiv. 14, 18, which combines rhythm of sound with rhythm of thought and well illustrates the form of the earliest popular Hebrew poetry:

Out of the eater came something to eat,

And out of the strong came something sweet,

And its answer: If with my heifer you did not plow,

You had not solved my riddle now.

Proverbs xxx. 15-31 contains a collection of numerical riddles, combined with their answers.

Proverbs are found in the oldest Hebrew literature. The Midianite kings, awaiting death at the hand of Gideon, cite a popular proverb, For as the man, so is his strength. David in his conversation with Saul says, As runs the proverb, "Out of the wicked cometh forth wickedness" (I Sam. xxiv. 13). Frequent references are also found to wise men and women, and examples are given of their prudence and insight Thus Joab, David's iron-hearted commander, brings a wise woman from Tekoa, the later home of the prophet Amos, to aid him in securing the recall of the banished Absalom. By her feigned story she succeeds in working upon the sympathy of the king to such a degree that he commits himself finally to a principle which she at once asks him to apply to the case of his own son (II Sam. xiv. 1-24).

The stories told in I Kings iii. 16-28, to illustrate the wisdom of Solomon, suggest the historical basis of the reputation which he enjoyed in the thought of succeeding generations. Such stories also indicate, as do the other early examples of the work of the wise, the conception of wisdom held in that more primitive age. Such wisdom does not necessarily include ethical righteousness or even practical executive ability, for the true Solomon of history was lacking in both; but rather a certain. shrewdness, versatility, and keenness of insight which enable its possessor to discern what is not clearly apparent. First Kings iv. 29-34 contains the later popular tradition of Solomon's wisdom:

(29) And God gave Solomon wisdom and insight in plentiful measure, and breadth of mind, even as the sand that is on the seashore, (30) so that Solomon's wisdom surpassed the wisdom of all the eastern Arabians and all the wisdom of Egypt. (31) For he was wiser than all men: than Ethan the Ezrahite, and Heman, Calcol, Darda, the sons of Mahol, and his fame was in all the surrounding nations. (32) And he uttered three thousand proverbs, and his songs were five thousand. (33) And he spoke of different varieties of trees, from the cedar that is in Lebanon even to the hyssop that springs out of the wall; he spoke also of beasts, of birds, of creeping things, and of fishes. (34) And there came some from among all peoples to hear the wisdom of Solomon, deputed by all kings of the earth, who had heard of his wisdom.

A popular proverb, like a primitive oral law, usually grows out of common human experience, and is gradually formulated and moulded into its final literary form by successive generations. No one man can claim it as his own, and even if he could, the ancient Semitic East, which cared so little about authors' titles, would have quickly forgotten his name. That Solomon did utter certain brilliant aphorisms, embellished by illustrations drawn from animal and plant life, cannot be doubted; and that some of them have been preserved in the book of Proverbs is probable. These facts and the popular tradition that tended to exalt his wisdom clearly explain why all Hebrew proverbs were attributed to him (Prov. i. 1), in the days of the final editing of the book of Proverbs.

That our present book of Proverbs is the work of many unknown sages, and consists of a collection of smaller groups coming from different periods, is demonstrated by the superscriptions which recur throughout the book, such as, These are the proverbs of Solomon (x. 1), These also are the sayings of the wise (xxiv. 23), These are the proverbs of Solomon which the men of Hezekiah king of Judah copied out (xxv. 5), The words of King Lemuel (xxxi. 1), The same proverbs also recur In different groups, indicating that originally they were independent collections, gleaned from the same field. When the first collection was made, the title Proverb of Solomonevidently meant a popular maxim handed down from antiquity and therefore naturally attributed to the most famous wise man in Israel's early history. It is an instructive fact that later proverbs, the immediate superscriptions to which plainly state that they come from many different sages, are still called Proverbs of Solomon; it betrays an exact parallel to the similar tendency, apparent in the legal and prophetic literature, to attribute late anonymous writings to earlier authors. This is also further illustrated by such late Jewish books as The Wisdom of Solomon or the Psalms of Solomon.

The individual proverbs confirm the general conclusion that they come from many different authors. Those which commend fidelity to one wife and kingly consideration for the rights of subjects, qualities in which Solomon was sadly lacking, do not fit in his mouth. Many are written from the point of view of a subject, and describe what a man should do in the presence of a ruler. Furthermore, the ethical standards upheld are those of prophets who lived and taught long after the days of the Grand Monarch who fascinated his own and succeeding generations by his brilliant wit rather than by his sterling virtues.

The book of Proverbs is far more than an epitome of his versatile sayings: it represents at least ten centuries of experience divinely guided, but won often through mistakes and bitter disappointments. It contains the many index hands, set up before the eyes of men to point them from error to truth, from folly to right, and from failure to success. Like most of the Old Testament books, it embodies the contributions of many different teachers writing from many different ages and points of view. Their common aim is well expressed by the sage who appended to Proverbs the preface:

To acquire wisdom and training,

To understand rational discourse,

To receive training in wise conduct,

In uprightness, justice, and rectitude,

To impart discretion to the inexperienced,

To the young knowledge and insight;

That the wise man may hear and add to his learning,

And the man of intelligence gain education,

To understand a proverb and a parable,

The words of sages and their aphorisms.

The structure and contents of the book suggest its literary history. Like the New Testament, it appears to have passed through different stages, and to have been supplemented repeatedly by the addition of new collections. The original nucleus is probably found in x. 1 to xxii. 16; this is introduced by the simple superscription,The Proverbs of Solomon. The form of the proverb is simple; the atmosphere is joyous, prosperity prevails, virtue is rewarded; a king who loves justice and righteousness is on the throne (xiv. 35, xvi. 10, 12, 13, xx. 8, xxii. 11); the rich, and poor stand in the same relation to each other as in the days of the pre-exile prophets; and the teaching of their prophets—righteousness is more acceptable than sacrifice—is frequently reiterated (xv. 8, xvi. 6, xxi. 3, 27). While this long collection doubtless contains many proverbs antedating even the beginnings of Israel's history and possibly some added later, the indications are that they represent the original edition of the book which the Jews carried with them into the Babylonian exile. This early collection was perhaps made under the inspiring influence of the reign of Josiah.

Undoubtedly the remaining collections also contain many very ancient proverbs, but as a whole their literary form and thought is more complex. The descriptions of the kings suggest the Persian and Greek tyrants who ruled over the Jews during the long centuries after the exile (cf. xxv. 1-7, xxviii. 2, 12, 15, 28, xxix. 2, 4, 16, xix. 14), The age of the prophets has apparently been succeeded by that of the priest and the law (xxix. 18). Already the Jews have tasted the bitterness of exile (xxvii. 8). There are also certain points of close contact with proverbs of Ben Sira, written about 190 B.C. The sages as a class are very prominent, as in the later centuries before Christ. These and many other indications lead to the conclusion that the different collections were probably made after the exile, and that the noble introduction, i.-ix., and the two chapters in the appendix were not added until some time in the Greek period, — not long before 200 B.C. The date, however, when these proverbs arose and were committed to writing is comparatively unimportant, save as a knowledge of their background aids in their interpretation, and as they, in turn, reveal the life and thought of the persecuted, tempted Jews, whose religious life centred in the second temple.

Probably in the Greek period also a poet-sage collected and wove together certain love and wedding songs of his race. The result was called the Song of Songs, that is, the Peerless Song. According to one interpretation, it presents, in a series of scenes, the heart struggle of a simple country maiden with the promptings of a true, pure love for a shepherd lover and the bewildering attractions of a royal marriage; and true love in the end triumphs. Whatever be the interpretation, it is clear that this exquisite little book, so filled with pictures of nature and simple country life, was intended to emphasize the duty and beauty of fidelity to nature and the promptings of the human heart. This thought is expressed in the powerful passage which seems to voice the central teaching of the poem:

Love is strong as death;

Jealousy is as cruel as Sheol;

Its flashes are flashes of fire,

A very flame of Jehovah.

Many waters cannot quench love,

Neither can floods drown it:

If a man would give all the substance of his house for love,

He would utterly be condemned.

XI
THE WRITINGS OF ISRAEL'S PHILOSOPHERS

An intense interest in man led certain of Israel's sages in time to devote their attention to more general philosophical problems, such as the moral order of the universe. In the earlier proverbs, prophetic histories, and laws, the doctrine that sin was always punished by suffering or misfortune, and conversely that calamity and misfortune were sure evidence of the guilt of the one affected, had been reiterated until it had become a dogma. In nine out of ten cases this doctrine was true, but in time experience proved that the tenth case might be an exception. While most of the teachers of the race denied or ignored this exception, certain wise men, faithful and unflinching in their analysis of human life, faced the fact that the innocent as well as the guilty sometimes suffer. Their quest for the answer to the eternal question, Why? is recorded in the books of Job and Ecclesiastes.

The basis of the book of Job Is undoubtedly a primitive story. Traces of a tradition somewhat similar have recently been discovered in the Babylonian-Assyrian literature. The Babylonian treatment of the moral problem that it presents is even more strikingly similar. Ezekiel also refers to a well-known popular Hebrew version of the story of Job (xiv. 14): though these three men, Noah, Daniel, and Job, were in it (the guilty land), they would deliver simply their own lives their righteousness, saith the Lord Jehovah (cf. also xiv. 20). Evidently in Ezekiel's day these names represented three ancient worthies, each conspicuous for his superlative piety. The Hebrew word here used also indicates that the righteousness attributed to them was conformity to the demands of the ritual. This agrees closely with the representation of the prose version of the story found in Job i. ii. and xlii. 7-17; here the supreme illustration of Job's piety is that he repeatedly sacrifices burnt-offerings, whenever there is the least possibility that his sons have sinned (i. 4, 5). Also in describing his perfection (i. 1), the same unusual term is employed as in the priestly narrative of Genesis vi. 9, where Noah's righteousness is portrayed.

It seems probable, therefore, that the ancient story of Job was committed to writing by some priest during the Babylonian exile. Since Job and his friends live out on the borders of the Arabian desert to the east or southeast of Palestine, it seems clear that the tradition came to the Hebrews originally from some foreign source; but in the prose form in which we find it in Job, it has been thoroughly naturalized, for Job is a faithful servant of Jehovah and the law. Ignoring for the moment the poetical sections (iii. 1 to xlii. 6), we find that the prose story has a direct, practical message for the broken-hearted exiles, crushed beneath an overpowering calamity. Jehovah is testing his servant people, as he tests Job in the story, to prove whether or not they fear God for nought (i, 9). If they bear the test without complaint, as did Job, all their former possessions will be restored to them in double measure (xlii. 7-17).

This prose story has apparently been utilized and given a very different interpretation by a later poet-sage in whose ears rang Jeremiah's words of anguish, found in chapter xx. 14-18 of his prophecy (cf. Job iii.), and to whose ears came also the cry of the pious voiced in Malachi ii. 17: Every one who does evil is good in the sight of Jehovah, and he delighteth in them. Where is the God of justice? The old solutions of the problem of evil were being openly discarded. They who feared Jehovahwere saying (iii, 13, 14), It is vain to serve God; and what profit is it to have kept his charge or to have walked in funeral garb before Jehovah of hosts? Even now we must congratulate the arrogant; yea, they who work wickedness are entrenched; yea, they tempt God and escape! With a boldness and thoroughness that must have seemed to his contemporaries dangerous and heretical, the great poet-sage presents the problem in all its intensity.

He adopts the popular story, utilizing it as his prologue and epilogue: but as we pass to chapter iii, the simple, pure Hebrew yields to sublime poetry, shot through with the words and idioms and ideas of a much later age. The designation of God is no longer Jehovah but El or Eloah or Shaddai. The character of Job suddenly changes; instead of being the patient, submissive servant of the law, he boldly, almost defiantly, charges God with injustice. The role of the friends also changes, and they figure as champions of the Deity. In their successive speeches they present in detail the current dogmas and the popular explanations of suffering. In his replies Job points out their inapplicability to the supreme problem of which he is the embodiment. The action and progress in this great drama is within the mind of Job himself. By degrees he rises to a clear perception of the fact that he is innocent of any crime commensurate with the overwhelming series of calamities which have overtaken him; and he thus throws off the shackles of the ancient dogma. From the seemingly cruel and unjust God who has brought this undeserved calamity upon him, he then appeals to the Infinite Being who is back of all phenomena.

The reply to this appeal, and the author's contribution to the eternal problem of evil, are found in xxxviii. I to xlii. 6. It is not a solution, but through the wonders of the natural world, it is a fuller revelation to the mind of Job, of the omnipotence, the omniscience, the wisdom, and the goodness of God. Even though he cannot discern the reason of his own suffering, he learns to know and to trust the wisdom and love of the Divine Ruler.

I had heard of this by the hearing of the ear;

But now mine eye seeth thee (xlii. 5).

Faith triumphs over doubt, and the problem, though unsolved, sinks into comparative insignificance. Apparently another poet-sage has added, out of the depths of his own experience, his contribution to the problem of suffering in the speeches of Elihu (chapters xxxii-xxxvii). It is that suffering rightly borne becomes a blessing because it is one of God's ways of training his servants. This indeed is an expansion of the explanation urged by Eliphaz in v. 17, Behold, happy is the man whom God correcteth. While these speeches of Elihu are written in a different literary style and have, in fact, no vital connection with the original poem of Job, they nevertheless contain a great and intensely practical truth; they have rightly found a place in this marvellous book. Similarly the sublime description of wisdom in chapter xxviii. makes good its title; it can, however, be studied best by itself apart from Job's impassioned protestations of his innocence (chapter xxix.).

Thus the book of Job, like so many other Old Testament writings, has its own literary history. Somewhere and sometime, back in an early Semitic period, there doubtless lived a man, conspicuous for his virtue and prosperity. Upon him fell a misfortune so great and apparently undeserved that it made a deep impression, not only upon his contemporaries, but also upon the minds of later generations. Thus there grew up a common Semitic story of Job which was in time thoroughly naturalized in Israel. Probably a Jewish priest in the exile first committed it to writing in order to assure his fellow-sufferers that could they but be patient and submissive Jehovah would soon restore them to their former prosperity. The painful experiences that came to the Jews, especially to the pious, during the middle and latter part of the Persian period (sometime between 450 and 340 B.C.), convinced a poet- sage that the old interpretations of the meaning of suffering did not suffice. Accordingly into the heart of the familiar story of Job he injected his powerful, impassioned message. Later writers, inspired by his inspiring genius, added their contributions to the solution of the perennial problem. Hence by 200 B.C., at least, the book of Job was probably current in its present form.

The same ever-recurring, insistent questions regarding the moral value and meaning of life led another later wise man to embody the results of his observation and experience in what we now know as the book of Ecclesiastes. Although i. 16 and ii. 7, 9 clearly imply that many kings had already reigned in Jerusalem, the author seems to put his observations in the mouth of Solomon, the acknowledged patron of wisdom teaching. The evidence, however, that the book is one of the latest in the Old Testament is overwhelmingly conclusive. The language is that of an age when Hebrew had long ceased to be spoken. The life mirrored throughout is that of the luxurious, corrupt Greek period. If not directly, at least indirectly, it reflects the doctrines of the Stoics and the Epicureans. It was a crooked, sordid, weary world upon which its author looked. It is not strange that a vein of materialism and pessimism runs through his observations and maxims. All is vanity is the dominant note, and yet light alternates with shadow. He loses faith in human nature; yet he does not give up his faith in God, though that faith is darkened by the desolateness of the outlook. While the book has practical religious teachings, perhaps its chief mission, after all, is vividly to portray the darkness just before the dawn of the belief in a future life and before the glorious rising of the Sun of Righteousness.

Its teachings naturally called forth many protests, explanations, and supplements, and these have found the permanent place in the book that they rightfully deserve. Its fragmentary structure and abrupt transitions also made later insertions exceedingly easy. These are the simplest and the most natural explanation of the sharp contradictions that abound in the book (cf. e.g., ii. 22 and iii. 22, or iv. 2 and ix. 4, or iii. 16 and iii. 17, or viii. 14 and ix. 2, or iii. 1-9 and iii. 11). The preacher, whose painful experiences and prevailingly pessimistic teachings are the original basis of the book, appears to have been consistent throughout. He ends in xii. 8 with the same refrain, Vanity of vanities; all is vanity! In a divine library like the Old Testament, reflecting every side of human thought and experience, such a book is not inappropriate. Its contradictions provoke thought; they beget also a true appreciation of the positive notes thus brought into dramatic contrast with the ground tones of pessimism which resound through all literature and history.

XII

THE HISTORY OF THE PSALTER

Corresponding to the book of Proverbs, itself a select library containing Israel's best gnomic literature, is the Psalter, the compendium of the nation's lyrical songs and hymns and prayers. It is the record of the soul experiences of the race. Its language is that of the heart, and its thoughts of common interest to worshipful humanity. It reflects almost every phase of religious feeling: penitence, doubt, remorse, confession, fear, faith, hope, adoration, and praise. Even the unlovely emotion of hatred is frankly expressed in certain of the imprecatory psalms. The Psalms appeal to mankind in every age and land because, being so divine and yet so human, they rest on the foundations of universal experience. Whenever a heart is breaking with sorrow or pulsating with thanksgiving and adoration, its strongest emotions find adequate expression in the simple and yet sublime language of the Psalter.

In the familiar doings of Mary and Zacharias, found in the opening chapters of Luke, we may trace the beginnings of the hymn literature of the early Christian Church, a literature which later became one of the Church's most valued possessions. If the canon of the New Testament had been closed in 1000 instead of 400 A.D., its books would doubtless have included a hymnal which would have corresponded closely to the Psalter of the Old. Just as the Psalms represent the application of the great doctrines of the Hebrew prophets in the spiritual life of the community, so this new hymnal would represent the personal application of the teachings of Jesus and the apostles to the religious life of the Church and the individual. The Psalter is also what it is because its background is a period of stress and severe trial. In the hot furnace of affliction and persecution the psalmists learned to appreciate the truths which they so confidently and effectively proclaim. Then the spiritual teachings of the earlier prophets, which were contemptuously rejected by their contemporaries, were at last appropriated by the community. The Psalter as a whole appears, therefore, to be one of the latest and most precious fruits of the divine revelation recorded in the Old Testament.

In its present form, the Psalter is divided into five books or collections. At the end of each collection there is a concluding doxology (xli., lxxii., lxxxix., cvi). The last psalm (cl.) serves as a concluding doxology, not only to the fifth collection, but also to the Psalter as a whole. Certain psalms are also reproduced in two different collections with only slight variations. For example, xiv. is practically identical with liii., except that in the first Jehovah is always used as the designation of the Deity, and in liii. Elohim or God; again Psalm xl. 13-17 is reproduced in lxx.; lvii. 7-11 and lx. 5-12 are together practically equivalent to cviii. These and kindred facts indicate that the Psalter, like the book of Proverbs, is made up of collections originally distinct. The division into exactly five groups appears to be comparatively late, and to be in imitation of the fivefold division of the Pentateuch.

The genesis of the book of Proverbs is exceedingly helpful in tracing the closely analogous growth of the Psalter. The prevailing form of the superscriptions and the predominant use of the name Jehovah or Elohim also aid in this difficult task. Psalms i. and ii. are introductory to the entire book. Psalms iii-xli. all bear the Davidic superscription and use the designation Jehovah two hundred and seventy-two times, but Elohim only fifteen. The form and contents of these psalms, as well as their position, suggest that they are the oldest collection in the book. In the Greek version all the psalms of the collection found in li-lxxii., excepting Psalm lxvi., which is anonymous, and lxxii., which is attributed to Solomon, have also the Davidic superscription. Although certain subsequent psalms are ascribed to David, as, for example, lxxxvi., ci., and ciii., the close of the collection, is the significant epilogue (lxxii. 20), the prayers of David the son of Jesse are ended.

Before the approximate date of these collections can be determined the significance of the Davidic title needs interpretation. In the Hebrew version, this title is borne by seventy-three psalms. Two are ascribed to Solomon (lxxii. and cxxvii.), one to Moses (xc.), and twenty-four to the members of the post-exilic guilds of temple singers. The superscriptions of the Greek and Syrian versions contain many variations from those in the

Hebrew. This is probably due to the fact that superscriptions are usually added by later scribes in whose minds the question of authorship first became prominent. In earlier Hebrew the phrase commonly translated Psalm of David would more naturally mean a psalm for David or dedicated or attributed to David. The latter appears to have been its original significance. Like the title, Proverbs of Solomon, it was used to distinguish an ancient poem, which, being a psalm, was naturally ascribed to David, and to him later Judaism, in common with the New Testament writers, attributed all psalm literature. A detailed study of the superscriptions soon demonstrates that the majority of them represent only the conjectures of scribes who were guided by current traditions or suggestions embodied in the psalms themselves. In this manner, to Solomon, the builder of the temple, is ascribed Psalm cxxvii., because it refers to the building of the house in its opening verse. The Greek version even attributes to David Psalm xcvi., which, it states, was writtenwhen the temple was being built after the captivity.

Since the superscriptions to the Psalter were only very late additions, the question still remains, What was the basis of the late Jewish tradition that makes David the father of the psalm literature, as was Solomon of the wisdom, Moses of the legal, and Enoch of the apocalyptical? The other Old Testament books give no direct answer. They tell us, however, that the warrior king was skilled in playing the lyre, and we are aware that to this, in antiquity, an improvised accompaniment was usually sung. We also have the account of David's touching elegies over the death of Saul and Jonathan and of Abner (II Sam. i., iii. 33, 34). Moreover, the early historical books vividly portray the faults of David, the limitations which he shared in common with his contemporaries, and his deeply religious spirit; but they leave the question of his relation to the Psalter to be settled by the testimony of the individual psalms. Here the evidence is not conclusive. It is clear that many of the psalms attributed by tradition to him were written in the clearer light of later prophetic teaching and amid very different circumstances from those which surrounded Israel's early king. Still it would be dogmatic to assert that nothing from his lips is to be found in the

Psalter; and to point out with assurance those passages and psalms which must be Davidic is quite as unwarrantable.

The Psalter is clearly the repository of that which was best in the earlier spiritual life and thought of the race. While there are no direct references to songs in connection with the pre-exilic Jewish temple, Amos (v. 23) found them in use at the sanctuary at Bethel; and from Psalm cxxxvii. 3, 4 it would appear that the exiles in Babylonia were acquainted with certain songs of Zion or songs of Jehovah. Treasured in the hearts of the people, and attributed, perhaps even by the time of the exile, as a whole to David, they constituted the basis of the earliest collections of psalms, which, as we have noted, practically without exception bear the Davidic superscription. The date of each individual psalm, however, must be determined independently on the basis of its own testimony, although the historical allusions are few and the data in many cases are far from decisive.

Just when the earliest collections, found in iii.-xli. and li.-lxxii., were made is a comparatively unimportant yet difficult question to decide. Probably the rebuilding of the temple in 516 B.C. was one of the great incentives. The example of the Babylonians, who possessed a large and rich psalm literature, may also have exerted an indirect influence. At least it is certain that the guilds of temple singers and the song service became increasingly prominent in the religious life of the Jewish community which grew up about the restored temple. The presence of alphabetical psalms, as, for example, ix., x., xxv., xxxiv., xxxvii., in the earliest collection suggests also the leisure of the exile. The historical background of many of these psalms is clearly the exile and the long period of distress that followed. They voice the experiences of the poor, struggling band of the pious, who, living in the midst of oppressors, found in Jehovah alone their refuge and their joy. Some of these psalms also reflect the prophetic teachings of Jeremiah (e.g., xvi., xxxix) and of Isaiah xl.-lxvi. In general their attitude toward sacrifice is that of the prophets:

For thou desirest not sacrifice;

Else would I give it.

Thou delightest not in burnt offering.

The sacrifices of God are a broken spirit;

A broken and a contrite heart, O God, thou wilt not despise.

Religion is defined in the terms of life and acts. Ceremonialism has not yet cast its chilling influence over the heart of the nation. Therefore the earliest collections may, with considerable assurance, be assigned to a date not later than the days of Nehemiah (about 400 B.C.).

Psalms xlii.-l. and lxxiii-lxxxiii. constitute a collection of Levitical hymns. If we may follow the indications of their superscriptions, they consist of two originally distinct groups, the one, xlii.-xlix., associated with and possibly at first collected and preserved by the post-exilic guild of temple singers, known as the sons of Korah, and the other, l., lxxiii.-lxxxiii., similarly attributed to Asaph, the guild of temple singers, mentioned first in the writings of the Greek period. In these two groups the priests and Levites and the liturgy are prominent. Psalms lxxxiv.-lxxxix. constitute a short Levitical supplement. The remainder of the Psalter is also made up of originally smaller collections, as, for example, the Psalms of Ascent or the Pilgrim Psalms (cxx.-cxxxiv.), and the Hallelujah Psalms (cxi.-cxiii. and cxlvi.-cl.). Some of the latter come perhaps from the Jews of the dispersion. Each collection appears to represent a fresh gleaning of the same or slightly different fields, incorporating ancient with contemporary psalms, and, as has been noted, not infrequently including some already found in earlier collections.

Certain of the psalms, such as lxxiv., lxxix., lxxxiii., seem clearly to reflect the horrors of the Maccabean struggle (169-165 B.C.). Later Jewish literature bears testimony that in the last two centuries before Christ psalm writing increased rather than decreased (cf. e.g., Psalms of Solomon). Certainly the experiences through which the Jews passed during the middle of the second century were of a nature to evoke psalms similar to those in the Psalter. The probabilities, therefore, are that the Psalter, in its final form, is, like the book of Daniel, one of the latest writings in the Old Testament. It was possibly during the prosperous reign of Simon, when the temple service was enriched and established on a new basis, that its canon was finally closed.

The fact that they all gather about a definite event in Israel's history, and probably antedate the majority of the psalms in the Psalter, explains why the little collection of lyrical poems, known as the book of Lamentations, never found a place beside the kindred psalms (e.g., Pss. xlii., xliii) in the larger book. Their theme is the Babylonian exile and the horrors and distress that it brought to the scattered members of the Jewish race. Their aim is prophetic, that is, to point out and confess the guilt of the nation and its dire consequences. They reflect the teachings of both Jeremiah and Ezekiel. While it is not strange that later tradition attributed the collection to the first of these prophets, its contents do not support the conjecture. Four out of the five poems are alphabetical, and distinctly different points of view are represented. Chapters ii. and iv. probably come from the middle of the Babylonian exile, and to the remainder must be assigned a still later period.

The Psalter, with its natural appendix, the book of Lamentations, was the song and prayer book of the Jewish community. A majority of the psalms, and especially those in the latter part of the book, were doubtless originally intended for liturgical use. Many, particularly where the first person singular is used, are to be interpreted collectively, for here, as often in the book of Lamentations, the psalmist is speaking in behalf of the community. Others have been adapted to liturgical ends. But in the final analysis it is the experience and emotions of the individual soul that find expression throughout all the psalms. Since these experiences and emotions were shared in common by all right-minded members of the community, it was natural that they should in time be employed in the liturgy.

Again, as we review the history of the Psalter, we are impressed with the many sides of Israel's life and human experience that it represents. Not one, but perhaps fifty or a hundred, inspired souls, laymen, prophets, priests, sages, kings, and warriors, have each clothed the divine truth that came to them or to their generation in exquisite language and imagery, and given it thus to their race and humanity. Successive editors have collected and combined the noblest of these psalms, and the Psalter is the result. The exact date of each psalmist and editor is comparatively unimportant, for though differing widely in origin and theme, they are all bound together by a common purpose and a common belief in the reality and the immediate presence of God. All nature and history and life are to them but the manifestation of his justice and mercy and love. In direct communion with the God whom they personally knew, they found the consolation and peace and joy that passeth all understanding, even though the heathen raged and their foes plundered and taunted them. To that same haven of rest they still pilot the world's storm-tossed mariners.

XIII

THE FORMATION OF THE OLD TESTAMENT CANON

Could we have studied the scriptures of the Israelitish race about 400 B.C., we should have classified them under four great divisions: (1) The prophetic writings, represented by the combined early Judean, Ephraimite, and late prophetic or Deuteronomic narratives, and their continuation in Samuel and Kings, together with the earlier and exilic prophecies; (2) the legal, represented by the majority of the Old Testament laws, combined with the late priestly history; (3) the wisdom, represented by the older small collections of proverbs; (4) the devotional or liturgical, represented by Lamentations and the earlier collections of psalms.

Even before all the Old Testament books were written, the work of canonization began; before the first large canon was adopted, the prophetic and priestly narratives, and with them the earlier and later laws, were combined. This amalgamation was the work of a late priestly editor. The Pentateuch and its immediate sequel, Joshua, is the result.

A study of these books makes clear the editor's method. Naturally he gave the late priestly versions the precedence. He placed, therefore, its version of the creation first,—a position that it well deserves. Probably as a result of this arrangement the older and more primitive prophetic version of Genesis ii. 4a-25 was somewhat abridged, for it begins with the picture of a level plain, watered by a daily mist, and is immediately followed by the account of the creation of man. Genesis iii. and iv. are taken entirely from the prophetic, and practically all of v. from the priestly, group of narratives. Confronted by two variant versions of the flood, he joined them together into a closely knit narrative; but all the elements of both versions are so faithfully preserved that when they are again separated, behold! the two originally complete and self-consistent versions reappear. The story of Noah, the first vineyard-keeper, in ix. 20-27, is taken entirely from the prophetic history, but in x. two distinct lists of the nations are joined together. All the story of the tower of Babel in xi. 1-9 is from the prophetic, while the genealogical list in the remainder of the chapter is from the priestly history. The patriarchal and subsequent narratives are likewise combined with, the same remarkable skill.

Thus the first six Old Testament books were given their final form. The method in general was the same as that followed by the authors of the First and Third Gospels in their use of Matthew's Sayings of Jesus and the original Mark narrative, or by the authors of Samuel, Kings, and Chronicles in their citations from the older sources. In his close fusion of three or four parallel narratives the editor's work resembled most closely that of Tatian, who thus combined the four Gospels in his Diatessaron. So far as we are able to observe, the final editor of the Hexateuch preserved, like Tatian, most of the material in his older sources, except where a parallel version verbally duplicated another. The prophetic and priestly narratives also followed lines so distinctly different that cases of duplication were comparatively few.

To the latest editor of the early narratives we owe the preservation of some or the oldest and most valuable sections of the Old Testament. In that age and land of perishable writing materials, the prevailing method of compilation was one of the effective means whereby the important portions of primitive records were handed down in practically their original form. It is well that we are beginning to understand its significance in the realization of the divine purpose. Important beyond words, although often overlooked, were the services of the faithful editors who without the slightest desire for personal glory or reward, other than the perpetuation of truth, carefully selected, condensed, and combined material gleaned from earlier and fuller sources. To them is due the marvellous preservation of our Old Testament, To the honored rôle of the prophets and apostles, therefore, let us add the anonymous redactors.

The final editors were the immediate precursors of those who formed the successive canons of the Old Testament. Indeed, between the work of the former and the latter there is no clear line of demarcation. A period shortly after 400 B. c. is the date usually accepted for the work of the final editor of the Pentateuch; the canonization of the law, which included these five books, is dated between 400 and 300 B.C. The real canonization of Israel's laws had, however, begun much earlier. The primitive decalogue, represented by Exodus xxxiv., and probably from the first associated with Moses, appears, in the earliest periods of Israel's history, to have enjoyed a canonical authority. The primitive accounts, in Exodus xix., of the establishment of the covenant by Jehovah with his people mark the real beginning of the process of canonization,—a process, that is, of attributing to certain laws a unique and commanding authority.

Likewise the successive civil, humane, and ceremonial decalogues appear from the days of the united kingdom to have occupied a similar position. Primarily this was probably due to the fact that each was based upon a divine torah or decision, received from Jehovah through the priestly oracle. The public reading and promulgation of the Deuteronomic laws in the days of Josiah, with the attestation of the prophets and the solemn adoption by the people, was an act of canonization far more formal than the final acceptance of the New Testament writings by the Council of Carthage.

The next great stage in the canonization of the law is recorded in Nehemiah x. Then the representatives of the Jewish community entered into a solemn obligation and took oath to walk in God's law, which was given by Moses the servant of God, and to observe to do all the commands of Jehovah our Lord and his ordinances and his statutes (v. 29.) This action appears to be the historical basis of the fanciful and incredible Jewish traditions concerning the work of the Great Synagogue and the authority of Ezra. The new law thus adopted was evidently the one gradually developed and finally formulated by the Jewish priests in Babylonia. It was accepted, as was the earlier Deuteronomic code, because it met the needs and appealed to the moral and religions sense of those by whom it was adopted.

To set completely aside the Deuteronomic lawbook and the primitive decalogue of Exodus xx.-xxiii., already in force among the Jews of Palestine, was impossible and unnecessary. Hence, as we have noted, it was the task of some editor of the next generation to combine these and the earlier prophetic histories with the late priestly law and its accompanying history. Naturally this whole collection was still called the Torah or Law and was at once accepted as canonical by the Jews. This step was also most natural because their interests all centred about the ritual, and for two centuries the dominant tendency had been to exalt the sanctity of the written law.

It is possible to fix approximately the date of this first edition of the Old Testament writings, since the Samaritans adopted and still retain simply the Pentateuch and an abbreviated edition of Joshua as their scriptures. Although Josephus, following a late Jewish tradition, dates the Samaritan schism at about 330 B.C., the contemporary evidence of Nehemiah xiii. 28 suggests that it was not long after 400. It is therefore safe to conclude that by 350 B.C. the first five books of our Old Testament had not only been singled out of the larger literature of the race, but were regarded as possessing a unique sanctity and authority.

As the name Law suggests, the chief reason for this was the fact that these five books embodied laws long since accepted as binding. The second reason was probably because they were by current tradition ascribed to Moses. The third, and not the least, was, doubtless, because they met the need felt by the community for a unified and authoritative system of laws and for an authentic record of the earlier history of their race, especially that concerning the origin of their beloved institutions.

Evidence that the Law was first canonized

The priority of the canon of the law is also proved by the fact that, although it contains some of the later Old Testament writings, it stands first, not only in position but in the esteem of the Jewish race. Furthermore, it became in time the designation of all the Old Testament canonical writings. The term Law is thus used in the New Testament (e.g., John x. 34, xii. 34; I Cor. xiv. 21), in the Talmud, and by the rabbis, indicating that the later groups of historical, prophetic, and poetical books were simply regarded as supplements.

The history of the canonization of the next group, known as the Prophets, is very obscurely recorded, and this largely because it reached its culmination in the Greek period, concerning which we have only the most meagre information. Here analogy with the history of the New Testament is helpful. The same influences which led the early Christians to add the Epistles and Acts undoubtedly operated upon the minds of the Jews. The Law represented only a limited period in their national and religious history. But the addition of the early prophetic and legal histories to the detailed laws prepared the way for the expansion of the canon. This included first, the four historical books, Joshua, Judges, Samuel, and Kings, with the exception of Ruth. These were designated as the Former Prophets. Thus even the later Jews recognized their true character and authorship. The second division of the Prophets included Isaiah, Jeremiah, Ezekiel, and the Book of the Twelve, which contained the minor prophets.

The order of the book and the probabilities of the situation suggest that the Former Prophets, since they were the immediate sequel of the prophetic histories of the Pentateuch, and recorded the deeds of such heroes as David, Solomon, and Isaiah, were added first. That they also bear the marks of late priestly revision, is direct evidence of the esteem in which they were held by the late priestly school that completed the canon of the Law. They therefore may have been added as early as 300 B.C. They were certainly known to the author of Chronicles, as his many quotations from them show, although it is difficult to see how he would have felt as free as he does to substitute the testimony of later tradition, if they were regarded as equally sacred with the Law.

The reference to the prediction of Jeremiah, in the opening verse of Ezra, suggests the reverence with which the author of Chronicles regarded the words of this prophet. The post-exilic Jews never ceased to revere the prophetic word. The popular belief, current in the Greek period, that the prophets had ceased to speak only deepened their reverence for the teachings of Moses' successors (Deut. xviii. 15-19). The devotion of the later scribes is evinced by the scores of glosses which they have added to the older prophecies. It is manifest, therefore, how strong was the tendency, even in priestly circles, to add the Prophets to the Law.

The process was probably gradual and perhaps not complete until the Jews had learned fully to appreciate the value of their ancient Scriptures, after martyrs had died for the sacred writings during the Maccabean struggle. Aside from supplements made to older books, as, for example, Zechariah ix.-xiv., the canon of the prophets was probably closed not later than 200 B.C. From direct evidence it is clear that the book of Daniel (written about 165 B.C.) did not find a place in this canon. It is also significant that in the prologue to the Greek version of Ben Sira or Ecclesiasticus (132 B.C.) the translator refers repeatedly — as though they were then regarded as of equal authority — to the Law and the Prophets and the rest of the books, or to the other books of the fathers. But most significant of all, Ben Sira, who wrote about 190 B.C., includes in his list of Israel's heroes (xliv.-l.) not only those mentioned in the Torah, but also David, Solomon, Hezekiah, and the chief characters in the Former Prophets. Furthermore, Isaiah and Jeremiah and Ezekiel are introduced in their proper settings, and the panegyric closes with a reference to the twelve prophets collectively, indicating that Ben Sira was also acquainted with the Latter Prophets as a group.

The reference to the rest of the books in the prologue to Ben Sira indicates that even before 130 B.C. certain other writings had been joined to the canon of the Law. Ben Sira himself, to judge from his description of David (cf. xlvii. 8, 9, and I Chron. 25), Zerubbabel, Joshua, and Nehemiah, was acquainted with the books of Chronicles, Ezra, and Nehemiah. Chapter xlvii. 8 apparently contains an allusion to a hymn-book attributed to David. Evidently he was also familiar with the book of Proverbs, including its introductory chapters. Thus we have a glimpse of the beginning of that third stage in the canonization of the Old Testament which, as in the case of the New, continued for fully three centuries.

The Psalter doubtless passed through different stages of canonization, as did the Old Testament itself. The earliest collection was, in the beginning, probably made for liturgical purposes, and its adoption in the service of the temple was practically equivalent to canonization. When successive collections were added, they too were thus canonized. The result was that the Psalter, when complete, enjoyed a position somewhat similar to that of the Law and the Prophets, although the authority of each rested upon a different basis. That the Psalter was early canonized is further demonstrated by a quotation in I Maccabees vii. 17 (about 125 B.C.) from Psalm lxxix. 2, 3, introduced by the words, as it is written in the Scriptures. This conclusion is also supported by the significant reference in the New Testament to the Law, the Prophets, and the Psalms (Lk. xxiv. 44). Jesus' use of the Psalter indicates that in his day its canonicity was already thoroughly established. Lamentations, by a late tradition attributed to Jeremiah, was probably also canonized contemporaneously with the Psalms.

The canonization of the book of Proverbs, like that of the Psalter, was undoubtedly by successive stages. The Jews of the Greek and Maccabean period were especially appreciative of this type of literature, and it was doubtless accorded its position of authority primarily because it rang true to human experience. That it was attributed to Solomon also told in its favor. Ben Sira's indirect testimony suggests that it and the books of Chronicles, Ezra, and Nehemiah, which were in close accord with the point of view of later Judaism, were already in his day associated with the Law and the Prophets.

The absence of any reference in Ben Sira to Daniel is significant. The first allusion to it comes from the last half of the second century before Christ. First Maccabees i. 54 appears to quote the prediction of Daniel ix. 27, and in I Maccabees ii. 59, 60, Daniel and his three friends are held up as noble examples of virtue. Thus it would seem that within a half century after the book of Daniel was written its authority was recognized. In New Testament times its canonicity is fully established (e.g., cf. I Cor. vi. 2, and Dan. vii. 22).

Concerning the canonicity of two books, Ecclesiastes and the Song of Songs or Canticles, the opinions of the rabbis continued to differ until the close of the first Christian century. From the Mishna we learn that the school of Shammai accepted Ecclesiastes, while that of Hillel rejected it. Finally, in a conference in Jamnia, about 100 A.D., the two schools finally agreed to accept both books as canonical. From Second Esdras and Josephus, however, we learn that the present Hebrew and Protestant canon of the

Old Testament had already for some time been practically adopted by common consent.

The last collection, which includes eleven books known as the Hagiographa or Sacred Writings, constitutes the third general division of the Hebrew Scriptures. It is a heterogeneous group of histories, prophecies, stories, and wisdom books. Some, like the Psalter, were, as we have seen, probably canonized as early as the Prophets; although the final canon of the Old Testament was not closed until 100 A.D. Even later the canonicity of Ecclesiastes, the Song of Songs, and Esther was sometimes questioned; most of them were regarded as authoritative as early as 100 B.C. Here, as in the case of the New Testament, the real decision was not the work of any school or council; but gradually, on the basis of their intrinsic merit, the twenty-four books of the Hebrew Bible were singled out of a much larger literature and recognized, at least by the Jews of Palestine, as the authoritative record of God's revelation through their race.

Jewish tradition, represented by Second Esdras xiv. and the Talmudic treatise Baba Bathra xv. a, states that all the canonical books were in existence in the time of Ezra. While the tradition is refuted by the historical facts, it appears to have influenced the Jews of Palestine in shaping their canon; since no books purporting to come from a later date or author are found in it. The broader-minded Jews of the dispersion, and especially Alexandria and the early Christian Church, refused to be bound by the narrow principle that divine revelation ceased with Ezra. Accordingly we find them adopting a larger canon, that included many other later writings known in time as the apocryphal or hidden books.

These consisted of three genuine works, — I and II Maccabees and Ben Sira or Ecclesiasticus; two didactic stories, — Tobit and Judith; four books wrongly ascribed to earlier authors, — the Wisdom of Solomon, Baruch, the Epistle of Jeremy, and Second Esdras (Gk. IV Esdras); and four additions to the Hebrew canonical books, — First Esdras, an expansion of the book of Ezra, the Prayer of Manasses, and additions to Esther and Daniel.

As is well known, these books were retained by the Christian Church, as they still are by the Roman Catholic and Greek churches, until the

Protestant reformers relegated them, as a whole, to a secondary place. Ultimately the Bible societies, during the first part of the last century, ceased to print them in the ordinary editions of the Bible. The result is that the present generation has almost forgotten their existence. The last decade or two, however, has witnessed a significant revival of interest among the scholars of Christendom, and the wholesome tendency to restore certain of the Apocrypha to the working Old Testament canon is very marked. This is only a correction of the error of the Protestant reformers in estimating the Apocryphal books, not by the intrinsic merit of each individual writing but of the group as a whole.

Some of the Apocrypha and kindred books like the apocalypse of Enoch, were quoted and recognized by New Testament scholars as having authority equal to that of the other Old Testament Scriptures. The rejection of I and II Maccabees and Ben Sira from the Palestinian canon because they were written after the days of Ezra and not associated with the names of any early Old Testament worthies, was due to a narrow conception of divine revelation, directly contrary to that of Christianity which recognized the latest as the noblest. These later Jewish writings also bridge the two centuries which otherwise yawn between the two Testaments—two centuries of superlative importance both historically and religiously, witnessing as they do the final development of the life and thought of Judaism and the rise of those conditions and beliefs which loom so large in the New Testament.

While they will always be of great value in the study of later Jewish history, literature, and religion, the majority of the apocryphal books undoubtedly belong in the secondary group to which the Palestinian Jews and the Protestant reformers assigned them. Three or four, however, tested by the ultimate principles of canonicity, are equal, if not superior, to certain books like Chronicles, Esther, and Ecclesiastes. First Maccabees records one of the most important crises in Israelish history. As a faithful historical writing, it is hardly equalled in ancient literature. Its spirit is also genuinely religious. The later but parallel history of II Maccabees is not the equal of the first, although its religious purpose is more pronounced. Its historical character, style, aim, and point of view are strikingly similar to those of the book of Chronicles. The proverbs of Ben Sira, while not all of the same value, yet abound in noble and practical teachings, very similar to those in the book of Proverbs. Not only does the Wisdom of Solomon contain many exalted and spiritual passages, but it is also of unique importance because it represents that wonderful fusion of the best elements in Hebrew and Hellenic thought which formed the background of Christianity. Probably the Church, will ultimately restore to its larger working Old Testament canon the beautiful Prayer of Manasses, already largely adopted in the prayer-book of the Anglican Church.

Our rapid historical study has revealed the unity and the variety of teaching reflected in the Old Testament, and has suggested its real place in the revelation of the past and its true place in the life of to-day. This older testament is the record of God's gradual revelation of himself through the history of the Israelitish race and the experiences and minds of countless men and women whose spiritual eyes were open and whose ears were attentive to divine truth. The same benign Father who has always spoken to his children has influenced them also to recognize the writings that most faithfully and fully record the spiritual truth thus revealed. Had the task been entrusted to our own or later generations, it is not probable that the result would have differed in any important essential. For a few brief centuries false theories and traditions may partially obscure the truth, but these, like the mists of morning, are sure in time to melt away and reveal the eternal verities in their sublime beauty and grandeur.

XIV

THE INTERPRETATION OF THE EARLY NARRATIVES OF THE OLD TESTAMENT

Of all the different groups of writings in the Old Testament, undoubtedly the early narratives found in the first seven books present the most perplexing problems. This is primarily due to the fact that they have been subject to a long process of editorial revision by which stories, some very old and others very late and written from a very different point of view, have been closely joined together. While there is a distinct aim and unity in the whole, in approaching them it is simplest to study each story as a unit in itself. Not only is this practical, but it is justified by the fact that almost every story was once current in independent form. Often, as in the case of the accounts of creation and the flood, it is possible to recover the older versions and even to trace their origin and earlier history.

The first essential, however, is to determine to the point of view and purpose of the biblical writer, who has taken the given story from the lips of his contemporaries and incorporated it in the cycle of stories in which it is now found, Here the language, literary style, theme, and conceptions of God and religion are the chief guides. If, as in the first chapter of Genesis, the Deity is always designated as God or Elohim; if the literary style is formal, repetitious, and generic; if the theme is the origin of an institution like the Sabbath; and if the Deity is conceived of as a spirit, accomplishing his purpose by progressive stages through the agency of natural forces, — it is not difficult to recognize at once the work of a late priestly writer. If, on the contrary, as in Genesis ii. 4b to iii. 24, Jehovah is the name of the Deity; if the style is vivid, picturesque, and flowing; if the interest centres in certain individuals instead of species; if the themes vitally concern the spiritual life of man; if the Deity is conceived of after human analogies, as intimately associating with men, and as revealing himself directly to them by word and visible presence, — the work of an early prophetic writer is evidently before us. The identification of the point of view of the author at once puts us into appreciative sympathy with him.

Value of knowing an author's point of view

It also enables us intelligently to interpret his words and figures. Knowing, for example, that the first chapter of Genesis was written by a priest who lived long after his race had ceased to think of God as having a body like a man, we cannot make the common mistake of interpreting verse 26 as implying physical likeness. Rather, as his conception of God as a spirit demands and the latter part of the verse proves, his sublime teaching is that man, the end and culmination of the entire work of creation, is like his Creator, a spiritual being, endowed with a mind and a will, and as God's viceregent, is divinely commanded to rule over all created things.

Where two distinct versions of the same narrative have been amalgamated in the process of editorial revision, the analysis of the original sources is indispensable to a true understanding and interpretation of the thought of the prophet and priest who have each utilized the ancient story,—as, for example, that of the flood,—to illustrate the inevitable consequences of sin and God's personal interest in mankind. Here the culminating purpose of the prophet, however, is to proclaim Jehovah's gracious promise that he will never thus again destroy man or living things; that (viii. 21, 22):

While the earth remains,

Seedtime and harvest,

Cold and heat,

Summer and winter,

Day and night

Shall not cease.

The priest, on the other hand, is interested in the renewal of the covenant which insures man's dominion over the natural world, and in the sanctity of blood, and in the primitive, divine origin of the command, Thou shalt not kill (ix. 1-6).

Fortunately the work of analysis has been so thoroughly carried out during the last century that there is practical agreement among the Christian scholars of the world on the essential questions. These results are now also available in popular form, so that, without wasting time on technicalities, the pastor and teacher of to-day can utilize them as the basis for more important study and teaching. The origin, the literary form, and the scientific and historical accuracy of each narrative all suggest definite and interesting lines of study, but, as has been noted (p. 106), these are of secondary value compared with the religious truths that each story is intended to illustrate.

Since these stories were preserved because they conserve this higher purpose, it is always safe to ask, What are their distinctive contributions to the grand total of ethical and spiritual teaching found in the Old Testament? At the same time it is exceedingly important always to be sure to read the teachings out of, and not into, a given narrative. By unnatural and fanciful interpretation of these simple stories the friends of the Bible in the past have often wronged it more than have its avowed foes. Each story, like the parables of Jesus, had its one or two central teachings, usually conveyed to the mind by implication rather than by direct statement. The characters who figure in them by their words and deeds proclaim the practical truths and embody the ideals in the minds of the ancient prophets and priests.

The heterogeneous group of stories found in Genesis i.-xi. constitute the general introduction to the succeeding narratives which gather about the names of the traditional ancestors of the Hebrews. Each of these originally independent stories illustrates its own peculiar religious teachings. None has taken a deeper hold on the imagination and made a deeper impression on the thought and literature of the world than that which is found in the second and third chapters of Genesis. Its theme— the origin and nature and consequences of sin—is of vital, personal interest to every man of every age.

The problem that confronted the early Judean prophet was to present in form intelligible to the minds of his primitive readers a subject that has taxed to the utmost the resources of the world's greatest philosophers and theologians. The task was comparable to that which fell to the Master when he sought to make clear to his untutored disciples the real nature of the mighty tempest of temptation that raged in his soul at the beginning, and, indeed, later in his ministry. The method adopted was strikingly similar in each case. If the language of modern philosophy and psychology had been at the command of these great religious teachers, it would have but obscured the great truths. These truths must be made objective; they must be expressed in the familiar language of the people. Even the inner struggle of conflicting motives must be presented in words so simple that a child could understand.

The second and third chapters of Genesis record the effective way in which a great early prophet dealt with his difficult problem. From the lips of the people he took fragments of ancient Semitic traditions. Almost all of the elements which enter into the story of man's fall have been traced to far earlier sources; but the narrative in its present unity and suggestiveness never has and never will be found outside the Bible. How far the prophet adapted to his higher purpose the current Hebrew version can not be absolutely determined. The fact alone remains that it is one of the truest bits of history in the Old Testament, and this not because it is a leaf from the diary of Adam and Eve, but because it concretely and faithfully portrays universal human experience.

In the simple language of popular tradition it proclaims, among other truths, that Jehovah, Israel's God, created man, breathing into him from his own nostrils the vital principle of life and making him the commanding figure in the universe; then that the Creator graciously provided all that was needful and best for his true physical and spiritual development. Incidentally the prophet calls attention to that innate and divine basis of the marriage bond which Jesus re-emphasizes (Matt. xix. 4-6). Physical death, according to the story in its present form, was not a necessary part of Jehovah's plan; the implication is that man would not die while he remained in the garden and ate of the life-giving tree. Temptation is not in itself evil, but necessary, if man is to develop positive virtue, for beside the tree of life grows the tree of the knowledge of good and evil, with its attractive, alluring fruit guarded by the divine prohibition.

The elements of the temptation are all presented in chapter ii., but the serpent, the craftiest of animals, in his conversation with the woman is required to make clear and objective the real nature of the conflict within her mind. The rôle of the serpent is the opposite of that of Balaam's ass, which figures in a story which comes from the same early Judean prophetic school. In the conversation between the woman and the serpent the true character of all temptation is revealed: it is the necessity of choosing between two courses of conduct neither of which is altogether bad. Curiosity, which is the guide to all knowledge, the beauty of the apple, which appeals to the aesthetic sense, and physical appetite, not in itself bad,—all these powerfully attracted the Oriental woman of the ancient story. On the other side she felt the compelling power of love and gratitude and the definite divine command.

The prophet saw clearly that all the elements of temptation are within man—a truth sometimes obscured in later Jewish thought. Milton has also led us astray in identifying the crafty serpent with the Satan of later Judaism. The prophet graphically presents another great fact of human experience, namely, that what is one man's temptation is not another's, that the temptation to be real must appeal to the one tested. The crafty serpent is not represented as speaking to the man; he would probably have turned away in loathing. His wife, she who had already sinned, the one whom Jehovah had given him as a helpmeet, herself appeals to the sense of chivalry within him. Hence the conflict rages in his soul between love and obligation to Jehovah and his natural affection and apparent duty to his wife. Thus in all temptation the diviner impulses struggle with those which are not in themselves necessarily wrong but only baser by contrast. Duty is the call of the diviner, sin is the yielding to the baser, motives.

The Hebrew word for sin, which means the missing of the mark set up before each individual, is the only altogether satisfactory definition of sin ever devised, for it absolutely fits the facts of human experience. Deflection from the moral standard set up by each man's conscience, even though his resulting act seem in itself noble, is for him a sin. Although the influences which led the man and woman of the story to disobey were exceedingly strong, the higher standard had been set up, and in falling short of it they sinned. Thus sin is not God's but man's creation, and results from the deliberate choice of what the sinner knows to be wrong.

In the same simple yet powerful way the prophet depicts the inevitable consequences of sin. At every point the picture is true to universal experience. The most appalling effect of a wrong act is that it destroys peace and purity of mind. It also makes cowards of brave men, and the presence and tender affection of the one wronged suddenly become intolerable. Sin also begets sin. To the cowering fugitives Jehovah comes, as he always does, with a message intended to evoke a frank confession which would tear down the hideous barrier that their sin had reared between himself and them; but, like most foolish, blind Adams and Eves, they hug their crime to their breasts and raise the barrier heaven high by trying to excuse their guilt. Thus they pronounce their own doom. For God himself only one course of action remains: it is to send them forth from his presence and from the life-giving tree, out into the school of hardship and bitter pain, that there they may learn the lessons which are necessary before they can again become citizens of the true Garden of Eden.

Two simple yet exceedingly significant touches lighten the gloom of this universal tragedy of human life. The one is that for the guilty, unrepentant pair, Jehovah himself made tunics of skins to protect them from the inclemency of their new life,—evidence that his love and care still went with them. The other is the implication that the true garden of Eden was still to be found on earth, and was closed simply to the guilty and unrepentant. The Bible is the record of how men learned the all-important lessons in the painful school of experience. Israel's teachers, each in his characteristic way, led their race on toward the common goal. The Gospels tell of how a man, tempted in all points as we are in a distant day and land found his way again into the abiding presence of God. He was one with the Father, not because he did not meet temptation in all its power, but because, unlike the actors in the primitive story, and all other participants in the drama of life, he yielded only to the guidance of divine impulses. Not content with achieving the goal himself, he gave his energies and his life to showing others how they also might overcome the baser impulses within them and find their way to God's presence and become one with him. Thus, because of what he did and said and was, he forever vindicated his title of Saviour of Mankind.

No other early Old Testament narrative is perhaps so full of rich spiritual suggestion as the one just considered, and yet each has its valuable contribution. Even such a story as that of the killing of Abel by Cain forcibly teaches the great prophetic truth that it is not the form of the offering, but the character and deeds back of the sacrifice, that determine Jehovah's favor or disfavor (iv. 7). Graphically it sets forth the spirit that prompts the greatest of crimes. In contrast to Cain, defiant yet pursued by haunting fear of vengeance, it also presents the divine tenderness and mercy in granting him a tribal mark to protect him from the hand of man. The similar story of Noah, the first vineyard-keeper, preaches the first temperance sermon in all literature, and also suggests the inevitable consequences of moral depravity so forcibly illustrated in the history of the ancient Canaanites. Even the prosaic table of the nations in Genesis x. emphasizes the conception of the unity of the human family which was destined in time to become the basis of Israel's belated missionary activity.

When we pass to the twelfth chapter of Genesis the independent stories coalesce into cycles, and each cycle, as well as each narrative, has its own religious purpose. In definite outlines each successive group of teachers painted the character of Abraham, the traditional father of the Israelitish race, and held it up before their own and succeeding generations as a perpetual example and inspiration. In the early Judean prophetic narratives he is pictured as the friend of Jehovah. His own material interests are entirely secondary, as illustrated in his dealing with Lot. Without hesitation he leaves home and kindred behind, for his dominating purpose in life is simply to know and do the will of Jehovah. To this end he rears altars throughout the land of Canaan. His chief joy is in communion with God and in the promises to be realized in his descendants. Through warring, hostile Canaan he passes unscathed, for his eyes are fixed on things heavenly.

It matters little whether or not, far back in the primitive days of Israel's history, a Bedouin sheik anticipated in actual character and life all that was gradually revealed to the prophets of a much later age. The supremely significant fact is that the noble ideal of Israel's earliest teachers was thus vividly and concretely embodied in the portrait of him whom the Hebrews regarded with pride and adoration as the founder of their race. In Hosea and Jeremiah, and less imperfectly in the nation as a whole, the ideal in time became an historical reality.

The early Ephraimite school of writers picture Abraham as a prophet (Gen. xx. 7), and therefore as an exemplification of their highest ideal. In the remarkable fourteenth chapter of Genesis he is a courageous, chivalrous knight, attacking with a handful of followers the allied armies of the most powerful kings of his day. Returning victorious, he restores the spoil to the plundered and gives a princely gift to the priest of the local sanctuary. In the later priestly narratives the picture suddenly changes, and Abraham figures as the faithful servant of the law, with whom originates the rite of circumcision, the seal of a new covenant (xvii). Later Jewish and Moslem traditions each have their characteristic portrait. One, which pictures him as in heaven the protector of the faithful, is reflected in the New Testament (Luke xvi. 23-30), Thus each succeeding age and group of teachers made him the embodiment and supreme illustration of its noblest ideals, and it is this ideal element that gives the Old Testament stories their permanently practical value.

Having noted the teachings that each individual story and the cycle as a whole conveyed to the minds of their first readers, it only remains for the teacher of to-day to translate them into modern terms. Some of the most important implications of the Abraham stories thus interpreted are, for example: (1) God calls each man to a high mission. (2) He will guide and care for those who are responsive. (3) To those who seek to know him intimately, and to do his will, he will reveal himself in fullest measure, and for such he has in store his richest blessings. (4) He that findeth his life (Lot) shall lose it, and he that loseth his life (Abraham) shall find it.

The Jacob and Esau stories contain marvellously exact and realistic portraits of the two races (the Israelites and the Edomites) that they respectively represent. Of the two brothers, Esau is in many ways the more attractive. He suggests the open air and the fields, where he loved to hunt. He is easy-going, ingenuous, and impulsive. His faults are those of not being or doing. As long as he had enough to eat and was comfortable, he was contented. He is the type of the world's drifters. Since Aram was far distant he disregards the wishes of his parents and marries one of the daughters of the land. No ambition stirred him and no devotion to Jehovah or to the ideals of his race gave content and direction to his life. Thus he remained a laggard, and the half-nomadic, robber people that he represented became but a stagnant pool, compared with the onrushing stream of Israel's life.

Jacob's faults are also presented by the early prophets with an astonishing fidelity. Rarely does a race early in its history have a portrait of its weaknesses as well as its strength held up thus prominently before its eyes. Jacob is the antithesis of Esau. While his brother was hunting care-free in the fields, he was at home plotting how he could farther his own interests. When the opportunity offers, he manifests a cold, calculating shrewdness. To make good the title to the birthright thus acquired he does not hesitate to resort to fraud and lying. Then he flees, pursued by his own guilty conscience, and, tricked by Laban, he serves as a slave fourteen years to win the wife whom he loves. At last, again a fugitive from the consequences of his own questionable dealing, he returns with quaking heart to face the brother that he had wronged.

The character is far from a perfect one, and yet the ancient stories suggest its elements of strength. By nature he was selfish and crafty; and yet he has what Esau fatally lacks: energy, persistency, and a commanding ambition. From the first his ambition looks beyond himself to the future of his descendants. Measured by our modern standards, his religious professions seem only hypocrisy; but as we analyze his character we find that a faith in Jehovah, narrow and selfish though it be, was ever his guiding star. Out of the tortuous windings of his earlier years it ultimately led him to a calm old age. Imperfect though his character was, like that of the race which he represented, the significant fact is that God ever cared for him and was able to utilize him as an agent in divine revelation.

Even more obvious and universal are the practical lessons illustrated by the Joseph stories. In the early prophetic narratives, Abraham is the perfect servant of God, Jacob the type of the Israelitish race, but Joseph is the ideal man of affairs. Graphically the successive stories picture the man in his making and reveal his true character. He is simple, affectionate, and yet strongly ambitious. His day-dreams make him odious, as in the case of many a boy to-day, to his unimaginative brothers. A seemingly hard fate rudely snatches him from the enervating influences of his childhood home and places him in the severe school of experience, where he is tested and trained. It also opens wide the door of opportunity. Fidelity to every interest and an unselfish response to every opportunity for service soon bring him into the presence of the Pharaoh. His judicious counsels, diplomacy, and organizing ability win for him the highest honors Egypt can confer. With modesty and fidelity he endures this supreme test — success. Toward his brothers, who had bitterly wronged him, he is nobly magnanimous, and to his kinsmen, who belong to the shepherd class especially despised as boors by the cultured Egyptians, he is loyal and considerate. Above all, not by professions, but by deeds, he reveals the true source of his strength, — a natural faith in the God of his race and an unfailing loyalty to him.

In the same way Moses, the exodus, and the great men and events of Israel's dramatic history, all have a religious importance and significance far surpassing the merely historical. At the same time the methods of modern literary and historical investigation reveal rather than conceal the deeper spiritual truths that they illustrate. The more light that can be turned upon them the more clearly will their essential teachings stand forth. Like the Old Testament as a whole, they grew up out of real life and truly reflect and interpret it, and therefore have a living, vital message to life to-day. Any interpretation that does not ring true to life may well be questioned. Finally, the authority of these ancient narratives depends not upon the historical or scientific accuracy of the individual story that is used as an illustration, but upon the fact that through the experiences and hearts of those who employed them God was seeking to make men free by the knowledge of the truth.

XV

PRACTICAL METHODS OF STUDYING THE OLD TESTAMENT

The Old Testament may be studied as literature, as history, as the record of an important stage in the evolution of religion, as the revelation of God to the race, or as a practical aid to the individual in living the true life. Each angle of approach calls for different methods and yields its correspondingly rich results. Studied in accordance with the canons of modern literary investigation, a literature is disclosed of surpassing variety, beauty, and fascination. After the principles of historical criticism have been vigorously applied, the Old Testament is found to contain some of the most important and authentic historical data that have come down to us from antiquity. To the general student of religion there is no group of writings that equals in value those included in these ancient Scriptures. As a simple, clear revelation of the character and will of the Divine Ruler, present and regnant in all life, the Old Testament is surpassed by only one other volume, and that is its complement, the New.

It is, however, as the guide to right thinking, and being, and acting, that the man of God may be perfect, completely equipped for every good work, that the Old Testament is and always will be studied by the majority of people. In so doing they will be realizing its primary and supreme purpose. Like true religion, it is not an end in itself, but simply an effective force, drawing and binding individual men to God and to the right. Any method of study that fails to attain this definite and practical end does not achieve the chief aim of the Old Testament writings.

This practical and personal end, however, cannot be attained at a leap. It is impossible to achieve the best results by taking a truth or a passage here and there and applying it at once to the individual. Both the Old Testament and the individual are something organic. Each book has a unity and a history that must be understood, if a given passage is to be fairly interpreted or its truths intelligently applied, Individual books are also related to others and to their historical background. Also, as has already been shown, to appreciate fully the vital message of a given writer it is necessary, not to know his name, but his place in history, his point of view, his method of expression, and his purpose. The Old Testament and Israelitish history as a whole are the best and most essential interpreters of individual books and passages. The most serious handicap to the ordinary Bible teacher and scholar is the lack of this broader, systematic, constructive knowledge. Much earnest, devoted study, especially in the Old Testament fields, is deficient in inspiration and results, because it is simply groping in an unknown land. It is all important, therefore, to ascend some height and spy out the land as a whole, to note the relation of different books and events to each other, and to view broadly the great stream of divine revelation which flows out of the prehistoric past on through the Old and New Testaments to the present.

In order effectively to apply the truths of the Old Testament to life, it is also necessary to regard the point of view of the individual to be taught. This fundamental principle of all education was fully appreciated and applied by Israel's great spiritual teachers. The result is that the Old Testament contains truths marvellously adapted to every age and type of mind. The importance of the religious culture of the child is emphasized by the comparatively large proportion, of writings especially fitted to hold the attention and arouse the imagination and shape the ideals even of the youngest. Nearly half of the Old Testament consists simply of narratives. Those inimitable stories, which come from the childhood of the race, have a perennial fascination for the child of to-day. They find him on his own mental and moral plane, as they did the primitive child, and by natural stages lead him on and up to the higher standards and broader faith of Israel's later prophets and sages, and thus prepare him to understand and appreciate the perfected life and teachings of Jesus.

In the modern use of the Old Testament, the faithful application of this fundamental principle also leads to a most practical conclusion; the stories peculiarly adapted to children are not the mature, legalistic narratives of the late priestly writers, but the early prophetic stories, which begin in the second chapter of Genesis. If children are taught only these, they will not be disconcerted by widely variant versions of the same events. Above all, they will be delivered from the inconsistencies and erroneous impressions which are often the cause of stumbling to the child. The later process of unlearning, which is always dangerous, will be avoided. If the problems presented by the priestly narratives be reserved until they can be studied from the broader and truer point of view, they will be readily solved, and the great positive teachings of these later didactic stories will be fully appreciated.

The subject-matter, therefore, supremely suitable for the earliest moral and spiritual culture of the child, is clearly the simple and yet profound prophetic stories of the Old Testament. It is very questionable whether the many excellent paraphrases now current are a gain or a hindrance. The ancient prophets and the generations who have retold them were inimitable story-tellers. To attempt to improve upon their work is futile. A simple, clear translation is all that is required. A Children's Bible is now being prepared according to the plan suggested above. The interpretation and application of their practical teachings can best be left to the intuition of the child and the direction of the intelligent parent and teacher.

It is also astonishing how readily even a little child appreciates the essential lessons, as, for example, those regarding the nature and consequences of sin, presented by the story of the Garden of Eden. Under the charm of the attractive personalities that figure in them, and the stirring achievements, so dramatically presented that they command breathless attention, the early prophetic narrations unconsciously and, therefore, all the more effectively, instil into the mind of the child the most essential truths regarding God and life and duty. At the same time, as they study in order the deeds of the heroes and makers of Israel's history, they are becoming familiar with the real background of the earlier revelation recorded in the Old Testament.

Therefore scattered throughout Genesis, Exodus, Numbers, Joshua, Judges, Ruth, Samuel, Kings, and the older sections of Ezra, Nehemiah, and I Maccabees, are to be found in rich profusion the material for the earliest years of Bible study. These should naturally be supplemented by the stories of the prophets, found in such books as Isaiah, Jeremiah, and Haggai. Their sequel and culmination are the corresponding stories in the Gospels and Acts.

In connection with the earliest study of the achievements of Israel's heroes and spiritual leaders, many of their greatest teachings would be appropriated and applied, but when the years of early adolescence are reached, the prophets in their sermons, the priests in their laws, the usages in their proverbs, and the psalmists in their psalms, each have certain personal messages, superbly adapted to the critical, formative years, when childhood begins to unfold into maturity. To make this material available, judicious selection and interpretation are required. The organism of each book and of the child must both be carefully regarded to make the adjustment perfect. Naturally this most vital line of study would be the introduction to a corresponding study of the direct, personal teachings of Jesus and the apostles.

This intensely practical work could profitably be preceded or followed by a study of the origin and growth of the different books and groups of Old Testament writings and the gradual stages whereby these Scriptures attained their present form and authority. The guides in this investigation should not be the Jewish rabbis or even the traditions of the Church Fathers. We have been misled too long by the pious guesses of the mediæval saints; but rather the testimony of the Bible itself and the evidence of contemporary writings should be the guides. The spirit should also be frank and constructive. The results cannot fail to be practically helpful in a great variety of ways. Thus on the basis of facts, in the light of history, and by the use of those methods of research which alone command respect and acceptance in other kindred lines of investigation, the questions which come to every thoughtful boy and girl will be fairly and truly answered. In this way those experiences which are inevitable in this critical age will deepen and broaden rather than destroy the foundations of individual faith.

With this general introduction, many students and classes will find it profitable to approach the Old and New Testaments from the distinctively historical point of view. Beginning with the unfolding of the civilization and religion of ancient Babylonia, they will study in conjunction the history, the strong personalities, the literature, and the thought of each successive period. The advantages of this method of study are many. Each book will be read and its messages interpreted in the light of the conditions and forces that constitute its true background. The different characters will live again, and the significance of their work and words will be fully appreciated as they are viewed in the clear perspective of history.

Above all, such a synthetic study of the unfolding of the supreme truths of revelation lays a foundation for the individual faith as broad as human experience. This is to attain one of the chief aims of all study, which is to put the individual into practical possession of all that is vital and best in the experiences and achievements of the past, that, thus equipped, he may go forth to fight the battle of life, valiantly and successfully.

This last course of study would call for several years, and, more than that, for enthusiasm, devotion, and real work. It would also take the student in time through the New Testament period, with its literature and commanding personalities and events, and perhaps beyond to the great epochs of Church history. Many would not stop until they had studied the latest chapter in Church history, the noble missionary activity and achievement of the past and present century.

When the Bible had thus been studied, the scholars in our schools would not be ready to graduate, but rather to enter upon that still deeper and more fundamental study which would mean an ultimate conquest of the broad field that it represents. Then it might be safe and profitable to adopt the topical method and study some one of the vital themes that are treated from many different points of view in the various parts of the Bible.

It will, however, probably be found easier and more natural next to take up in succeeding years the detailed study of the nine or ten great groups of writings which are found in the Bible. The natural and easiest method of approach to those of the Old Testament would be through a careful, constructive study of the history of the Israelitish race, perhaps beginning with the definite historical period of Saul and Samuel and concluding with the advent of Rome. Far better than any modern history of Israel is that marvellous history written by its own historians, which begins with the book of Samuel and ends with I Maccabees. Analyzed and arranged in their chronological order, these narratives tell the story with rare fascination and suggestiveness. Volume II of the "Student's Old Testament": contains the narratives from Samuel through I Maccabees, thus arranged.

On the basis of this detailed study of the historical background, the work and teachings of the prophets could next be traced in their true and chronological order. No Old Testament field is more neglected and none is more intensely interesting, when once the student understands the problems and aims of each great prophet. None has a more practical message for to-day, provided its supreme truths are interpreted into modern terms and conditions. After becoming intimately acquainted with the Hebrew prophets, it would be possible to go back and study with a new understanding and appreciation the early narratives which gather about the beginnings of Hebrew history. Then the intricate problems of the first eight books of the Bible would vanish in the light of a fuller knowledge. Above all, that which is essential and permanent would stand out in clear relief.

From the earliest fruits of prophetic activity it would then be profitable to turn to the later, represented by Lamentations and the Psalter. Here the best results require a classification of the different psalms according to their themes, so that their teachings can be studied systematically and as a whole. In this field of study the student comes very close to the heart of the Old Testament and the heart of the God who speaks through it.

Less spiritual and yet intensely interesting and practical is the great department of the Old Testament known as the wisdom literature. He that walketh with the wise shall be wise (Prov. xiii. 20) is as true to-day as when first uttered. This literature is a great mine of truth, almost entirely neglected by the Christian world. Systematic classification is the first requisite for the profitable study of the Proverbs and the later Wisdom of Ben Sira. From these the student may pass on to the fuller treatment of the omnipresent human problem, so sublimely presented in the book of Job, and to the many fundamental questions raised by Eccleslastes and the Wisdom of Solomon.

Last of all a year might well be spent in the study of the unfolding and concrete application and illustration of Israel's ethical and religious principles in the legal codes and institutions of the Old Testament. Many of these have found a higher expression, some are but symbolic, but others still have permanent authority and value. Studied as a whole and on the basis of a logical classification, this little understood field would also cease to be a jungle, and Instead would yield its own practical spiritual fruits.

XVI

RELIGIOUS EDUCATION – THE FUNDAMENTAL PROBLEM OF TO-DAY

This very brief and fragmentary outline of methods and possibilities of Old Testament study is not an impossible dream. In colleges and in a few Bible schools it is already being tried with the gratifying results that might be anticipated. To put it at once into force in most of our Sunday-schools would be absolutely impracticable. It is presented simply as a suggestion of a definite and practical goal toward which to work. With careful adjustment, these courses, adapted to different ages, could be arranged so that at least the intermediate grades in the Sunday-school would be studying in the same field at the same time. This plan provides for no graduation from the school of the Bible. It assumes that the Christian world is at last awakening to the real significance of religious education and to a recognition of the fact that the ultimate solution of our gravest national and social problems is to be found only in the inculcation of the true ethical ideals in the mind of the individual. It also assumes the fundamental principle that no worthy ends can be attained without real work, enthusiastic devotion, systematic methods, and above all a definite and worthy goal. It rests on the belief that the sense of gradual conquest and the attainment of practical results will alone inspire permanent devotion and evoke faithful work, and in the end prepare the individual scholar for the intelligent and loyal service of God.

Frank confessions are good for a cause as well as for the soul. We must admit that most of our Sunday-schools, with their vast resources in opportunity, in financial support, and in the devotion of the teachers and officers, do not permanently hold their scholars, and in the great majority of cases do not give them a thorough or systematic knowledge, even of the most vital teachings of the Bible. The ignorance of its literature and history on the part of even, the more intelligent students who enter college, is almost past belief, as many of us can testify from personal observation. The limitations in time and equipment of the Sunday-schools are undoubtedly great in comparison with those of the secular schools; and yet the responsibility now thrown upon the Bible schools is even greater than upon the latter. Parents have ceased to instruct their children in spelling and the multiplication-table because they have found that the teachers can do this better. Without justification, but by analogy and because they are themselves often unacquainted with the Bible, or uncertain regarding its interpretation, they are more and more leaving the religious education of their sons and daughters to the Church and the Sunday-school.

It is safe to say, and this without reservation, the most fundamental problem in England and America to-day is the problem of religious education, because this lies at the roots of all else — political, social, and theological. When the Christian world awakens to its profound significance, and when its ideals and methods are raised, even to a level with those of the public schools, the other grave problems will be near their solution. If the individual is thoroughly taught during the impressionable years of childhood and youth, the fundamental principles of ethics and religion, society and the state will have no difficulty in meeting their problems; but if not, these will perforce continue to remain unsolved.

It is a time for all earnest men of every denomination or creed to unite in meeting this need. In the Old Testament, Jew and Christian, Catholic and Protestant, stand on common ground. The modern inductive historical methods of study have prepared the way for union; for they aim to support no denominational interpretation, but simply to attain the truth. The last reasons, therefore, why the literature, history, geography, and ethical teachings of the Old Testament should not be taught in our public schools are rapidly disappearing, and the hundreds of reasons why any system of secular education is incomplete without it are coming to the front. With this fundamental basis of knowledge and instruction, the work of the Sunday-schools could also at once be placed on a far more effective plane. It is a consummation for which every intelligent citizen should earnestly work.

The achievement of the last century was to complete the work of the Protestant Reformation and rediscover the Bible. The task of the present century is to instil its essential teachings, thus revealed, into the mind of the individual, so that they will become controlling factors in human life. Here lies the great responsibility and opportunity of the Christian Church. If it is to renew its hold on modern men, it will be through the mind as well as the heart, and its most efficient method will be—as it always has in reality been—religious education. Horace Bushnell proclaimed the watchword of the Church triumphant: "Christian culture."

His, however, was no new discovery. The Hebrew prophets, priests, and sages were not primarily preachers, but teachers. The prophetic messages which fell on deaf ears, instilled into the minds of a few humble disciples, in time won acceptance from the nation. Jesus himself was not so much the preacher as the Great Teacher. His earliest public preaching was but the net cast to catch the few faithful disciples. When these had been secured, he turned his back upon a popular preaching ministry, and devoted the best part of his brief public work to instructing a little group of disciples. History completely vindicates the wisdom of his method. Only by following closely on his footsteps can the Church hope to realize its true mission, especially in this age, when the heart and will must be reached through the mind. In this respect, it must also be confessed that the Catholic are far in advance of the Protestant churches and Sunday-schools, where the preaching still overshadows the teaching.

To inspire and direct thorough religious instruction, carefully trained leaders are needed. The demand to-day is for a teaching as well as a preaching ministry, with an apostolic sense of a mission and a message. Men with natural gifts and the most thorough preparation are wanted to raise the standards and to organize and transform, as they alone can, by personal contact, the teaching corps of our Sunday-schools into effective forces. Such men and women certainly can be found. It is a conviction, based on a wide experience, that many of the ablest students in our colleges and universities, who for many valid reasons do not feel the call to a preaching mission, would gladly and enthusiastically devote themselves to the work of religious instruction, could they be sure of a field, when their preparation was complete. Our universities and seminaries already have the facilities and could readily assume this important responsibility.

As soon as our large city churches and the federated churches in our smaller towns, demand a teaching pastor as the permanent director of their Sunday-schools, and of the religious educational work under their charge, they will enter upon a new career of permanent conquest. The needs are undoubtedly great, the volunteers are at hand, thorough preparation can be assured; but the call must come from the Church, united and awake to its supreme opportunity and responsibility.

It must also be confessed that our religious systems – if such they may be called – are still in the experimental stage. They are far inferior in every respect, except in the self-sacrificing devotion of the teachers and officers, to those of the secular schools. What is most vital to our national and individual life is most neglected. Instead of the latest and best pedagogical methods, the most antiquated largely prevail. Saddest of all, the Bible which is being taught in the majority of our schools is the Bible of later Judaism and the Middle Ages, not the Book of Books which stands forth in the light of God's latest revelation, as a message of beauty and life to the present age. It is not strange that there is a growing distrust of the Sunday-school among many intelligent people, and an appalling apathy or distaste for Bible study in the mind of the rising generation.

If we shut our eyes to these facts, they will remain; but if we frankly face them, a decade of intelligent and devoted work will effect a great transformation. The first step is obviously along the line of improved courses and methods of study. Many different courses are at present in the field. All have their merits, and to those who have developed them highest praise and credit is due. Some have been prepared to meet immediate and practical needs, but ignore the larger unities and the historical background, and in general neglect the results of modern educational and biblical knowledge. Some have been worked out in the study and have a strong academic flavor, but do not meet the needs of the average scholar or teacher. Others are models of pedagogical perfection, but lack content. Progressive Sunday-schools are trying one system after another, and meantime the note of discontent is rapidly rising. The crisis is too serious to admit of personal rivalries or prejudices.

The moral of the situation is simple: that which will fully meet the needs of the present must be a combination of all that is good in existing courses, and embody what is best in the scholarship and methods of to-day. Like the most effective systems in the past, it must be wrought out in the laboratory of practical experience. It must be planned from the point of view of actual needs and conditions. It must also have a worthy and definite goal and a high ideal. It should emphasize the importance of fundamental religious instruction, as well as preaching. All that is practical and permanent in modern educational methods should be utilized. It should preserve the existing superb Sunday-school organization, and, as far as possible, the unity of the splendid system now under the direction of the International Committee. Finally, it should incorporate the positive and illuminating results of modern constructive biblical research. The task cannot be accomplished in a moment, nor by one man nor a small group of men. It is certainly important enough to command the best experience, the ripest scholarship, and the most unselfish devotion.

When this task has been thoroughly performed, and the ablest of our educated men and women have been enlisted in our Bible schools, the cause of religious education will command the respect of the world, not merely because of the fundamental need which it aims to meet, but also because it is effectually meeting it. The Christian Church will also find itself in sympathy and touch with that which is best and most significant in modern life and thought. Religious teachers and scientific investigators will work shoulder to shoulder in a common study and interpretation of God's many-sided revelation. Pastors will feel the solid foundations of historical truth beneath their feet. Leaving behind the din and distractions of the transitional period, the disciples of the Great Teacher will go forth with fresh zeal to make the eternal truths of the Bible regnant in the lives of men, and the kingdom of God a reality in human history.